Healing Pastors & People Following A Sheep Attack

By

Dennis R. Maynard, D. Min.

Illustrated By Chris Koonce

Copyright, ©2013

Printed in the United States of America. All rights reserved. No part of this book may be reproduced or transmitted in any form or by any means without written permission of the author.

Dionysus Publications
www.Episkopols.Com
49 Via Del Rossi
Rancho Mirage, California 92270

Email: Episkopols@aol.com

Telephone: 760.324.8589

ISBN: 13: 978-1484085554

Dionysus Publications
Books For Clergy And The People They Serve.
www.Episkopols.com

Cover Design
By
Chris Koonce

Chris Koonce resides in Fort Worth, Texas. He has designed several of the covers for my books. He is a very talented young artist. Chris earned a Bachelor of Fine Arts degree in 1991 from the University of North Texas. I encourage you to visit his website to view his portfolio of artwork. There are several opportunities for personalized gifts for yourself and others. He can also be a resource for fundraising opportunities for your organization, parish or school. Please visit his website.

www.kcfunart.com

Look for *Wilber's Wings: A Dog's View From Heaven,* being co-authored by Chris and me, to be released in the winter of 2013.

A bad dog trying to be good while learning all the power and responsibility that comes with being an angel.

*"It has been said 'time heals all wounds.'
I do not agree. The wounds remain.
In time, the mind protecting its sanity,
covers them with scar tissue
and the pain lessens.
But it is never gone.*
Rose Kennedy

THIS BOOK IS DEDICATED TO YOU

If you are a senior minister, music minister, minister of education or faithful lay leader that still suffers with the wounds inflicted on you by a handful of antagonists, my prayer is that this book will assist you with your healing. If years later you still wake in a cold sweat shaking from a nightmare filled with abusive memories, this book can help you. If you feel empty spiritually and unappreciated by the very Church you felt called to serve, this book will comfort you. You are the reason for this book. The stories shared on the following pages may sound just like your own. You are not alone. With each page you will discover just why I've dedicated this book to you.

Table of Contents

SECTION ONE
YOU ARE NOT ALONE

Chapter 1
From Shock To Sadness - 15

Chapter 2
Wounded Lay Professionals - 31

Chapter 3
The Congregation Will Be Wounded - 42

Chapter 4
Healing A Broken Parish - 60

SECTION TWO
THERE WAS NOTHING MORE YOU COULD DO

Chapter 5
Controlling The Narrative - 71

Chapter 6
The Antagonists' Preferred Target - 84

Chapter 7
No Apology – No Repentance - 93

Chapter 8
Objects May Appear Holier - 102

SECTION THREE
UNDERSTANDING WHY THEY DO IT HELPS A LITTLE

Chapter 9
  Spiritual Warfare - 111

Chapter 10
  Why Do They Do It? - 118

Chapter 11
  Antagonists Are In Pain - 131

SECTION FOUR
HEALING BRINGS NEW LIFE

Chapter 12
  The Severely Wounded - 143

Chapter 13
  Healing - 161

Chapter 14
  One Last Bitter Pill - 175

Chapter 15
  Remaining In Parish Ministry -187

Chapter 16
  Recovery and Resurrection - 196

About the Author - 207

Books By Dennis R. Maynard - 215

With Gratitude

Over the past twenty-five years my ministry in the larger Church has evolved. It began with requests from some of my clergy friends to lead their vestry or board planning retreats. Those retreats blossomed into larger conferences for rectors, staffs and schools. Then I began receiving calls to assist clergy that found themselves in conflicted congregations. Occasionally these requests came from their bishops. Far too often I discovered that the classical tools of conflict management were of no assistance. Then I began to realize that their several situations sounded eerily similar. In each case they had also been irresolvable. My role changed from consultant to pastor. For well over a decade now my ministry has become that of pastor to pastors, other Church professionals and lay leaders that have been wounded by a phenomenon that I have labeled as a *"Sheep Attack"*.

Analyzing the congregational system that allows pastors to be bullied was the obvious place to begin. The pattern of dysfunctional behavior became apparent. Only the names of the parties involved needed to be changed. There was an occasional tweak in the routine. Consistently, however, the pattern remained. Discovering ministers who had successfully survived an attack and remained in their congregations was more difficult. The greater challenge has been to find the ointment that would heal the injuries of those left bleeding at the doors of the Church.

"How will I ever get over this?" *"What am I supposed to do now?"* *"Will I be able to get another job?"* Those questions or ones very similar to them are the motivating reasons for this book. This is my attempt to continue to be a pastor to the countless victims of a nightmare that was not their choosing.

There is one insight I discovered in my research for this book that needs to be acknowledged. The victims of a sheep attack often share some of the same emotions as victims of physical and sexual abuse. There is a sense of shame and embarrassment. Talking about the event is difficult for them. The ideals that called them into ministry have been bashed on an ugly rock. The attacks go to the very heart of a pastor's identity and integrity. When those are destroyed their very moral authority, which is the keystone for ministry, is destroyed. This leaves them feeling alone and isolated. The pain is multiplied when they are marked as an outcast by the very Church they had considered family.

A critical part of their healing is to hear themselves talk about their abuse. Often, their bishops or denominational authorities placed them under *"gag orders"*. They were forbidden to do the very thing they need to do to begin the healing process. That is the case with several of the stories revealed on the following pages. To protect these few I have once again chosen to honor the anonymity of all.

My prayer is that this book will be an instrument of healing. The goal is to assist clergy, music ministers, other lay professionals and lay leaders to move successfully through the various stages of healing. That requires more than an exercise in listening. Having the pain they experienced validated by others is a first step. Reading the experiences of their fellow sufferers can help overcome feelings of isolation and loneliness. Sadly, those are only the first steps on a long journey to recovery. Their wounds are deep. Time will help, but the memory will always be with them.

Each week I receive another email, letter or telephone call from yet another victim of this brutal behavior. They have now come from virtually every state in the Union, Canada, and England. These stories appear to be unending. For that reason alone this particular book has taken several years to write. Each new story reassured me that a book like this is sorely needed. Ultimately it has required that I make peace with the fact that a book like this will never be finished. Letting go of the work I've done thus far and making it available for reading has been the toughest part.

Any artist can paint a portrait of a battle. A great artist can cause you to feel the pain that those engaged in the battle are suffering. A sheep attack not only leaves the pastor and their family in pain, but many members of the congregation will be wounded as well. This book does not deny or attempt to rationalize that pain. On the following pages the suffering will be well documented. Suffering has to be acknowledged before there can be healing.

I am grateful to all those who have allowed me to be their pastor. I am most indebted to those who gave me permission to share their stories. Without them I would not have been able to publish this work. While the larger Church appears to continue in a state of denial, those who have been through a sheep attack know otherwise.

I owe so much to so many. I am particularly indebted to Dr. John M. Evosevich, Ph. D. of Palm Springs, California for pointing me to the work of James Masterson, M.D. and Sam Vaknin, Ph. D. on Narcissistic Personality Disorder. I remain equally appreciative for the continued guidance that David Burgdorf of the Betty Ford Center in Rancho Mirage, California has provided me.

As I did with *"Preventing a Sheep Attack"* I asked a clergy panel to respond to the outline draft for this particular book. Their suggestions have done much to make this a better study. In particular I am thankful for the gifts and ministries of The Reverend Elizabeth Kaeton of the Canterbury Pastoral Care Center in Harbeson, Delaware, The Reverend Michael Russell of Austin, Texas, The Reverend Doctor Richard Sanders of Nashville, Tennessee, The Reverend Liz Zivanov of Honolulu, Hawaii, The Reverend Suzanne Watson of San Diego,

California and The Very Reverend Jonathon Jensen of Little Rock, Arkansas.

I remain grateful to each of you and all those, like you, who continue to read and utilize my endeavors. I am humbled and most grateful when you recommend my work to others.

May the Almighty continue to fill your life with blessings both seen and unseen.

Dennis R. Maynard, D. Min.
Rancho Mirage, California

Find Me On Facebook.
Dennis R. Maynard

IN SPANISH
To Be Released Fall, 2013

SECTION ONE

You Are Not Alone

"You are a priest forever, in the order of Melchizedek."
Hebrews 7:17

Chapter 1

From Shock To Sadness

Steele recalled his ordination at Saint Paul's Cathedral in Oklahoma City. There were seven of them being ordained that day. They stood before the bishop at the high altar. Together they responded to the Prayer Book vows. Then together they prostrated on the Cathedral floor before the bishop as he and the choir chanted the "Veni Creator.... Come Holy Ghost our souls inspire..." The words of the ancient prayer invoking the Holy Spirit burned into Steele's soul. He prayed that the Holy Spirit would be his constant companion in ministry and guide his every word and deed.

The bishop stared deep into his eyes before laying his hands on Steele's head. It was at that moment that all doubt was shaken from Steele Austin's soul. He knew beyond a shadow of a doubt he was answering God's call. He was fulfilling his destiny. He was put on this earth to be a priest. **Excerpt from the novel, *Behind The Magnolia Tree,* by Dennis R. Maynard, Dionysus Publications at Episkopols.com.**

I have lost count of the number of ordinations to the priesthood I've attended. In every one of them there is a moment that stands out. At some point in the service the ordinand's eyes will fill with tears. The eyes of many of the clergy ordaining the new priest will do the same. Often it comes during the laying on of hands or when the bishop hands the new priest a Bible and reminds them. "*Receive this Bible as a sign of the authority given you to preach the Word of God and to administer his holy Sacraments* (Book of Common Prayer – page 534)." No new clergy person gets to this point in their life easily. Many have fought with that intuitive little voice inside them for years or even decades. Once they yield to what they discern as God's call to ministry they still have a long struggle before them. They have to convince other clergy, church boards, diocesan and conference executives and psychiatrists that not only are they called to ministry but also are suitable for it.

      This is followed by three years of grueling study in a graduate theological school in addition to their college degree. They burn the midnight oil reading thick books and writing long papers on the various aspects of the Faith. Most must master either the Hebrew or Greek languages and prove competence in them. They must write a thesis that is without error of any kind and then defend it before a faculty panel. Once that is completed there are even more examinations by a bishop, diocesan committees, and more psychiatrists.

It's not the process that brings them to tears. It is the ultimate yielding to God's will in their lives. The ancient rite of "laying on of hands" is the final moment in the process. Now they are charged with preaching the good news of the resurrection of Jesus. Now they are to pastor people in the good and bad times in their lives. Now they are charged with forgiving sins, blessing marriages, comforting the sick and dying, and building up the Church, the visible Body of Christ on earth.

A sheep attack brings all that into question. For pastors being bullied into resigning from a parish it is not as simple as leaving one job in order to find another. The trauma of the attack calls the pastor's very identity into question. Clergy enter the ordained ministry filled with the ideals of the Gospel. They want to make a difference. They want to be a source of help and comfort. They are enthusiastic about bringing the love and presence of Christ into the lives of those they serve. The trauma of the attack shatters their idealism and pours doubt over their ability to accomplish their very life's mission.

The Loss of Identity and Integrity

I still don't understand what happened. Everything was going so well. The parish was in decline when they called me. The parish profile listed evangelism and stewardship as their primary need. It wasn't easy, but we started growing. Young families were joining the parish. We had to open a nursery. Something the parish hadn't needed in years. Our pledge income was up almost thirty percent. I thought I was in a happy place. The bishop called me on the telephone one afternoon. He told me that some very mean spirited people in the parish had contacted him. They wanted to audit my discretionary fund. They were questioning my financial management of the parish. He cautioned me to be careful. In just a matter of weeks both my wife and I were subjected to blackmail, death threats and physical actions that could have injured us if they had been successful. We were able to identify the three men that had targeted us. The rest of the parish was very supportive, but we just didn't think we could trust that group not to actually hurt us. I resigned. They immediately began spreading rumors that I had been stealing from the parish. Sadly, some in the parish believed them. Dennis, that was only a few weeks ago. My wife and I are still in shock. Your book has helped us to understand that we are not alone. But the thought of going back into a parish is terrifying. I not only lost a job, but I fear I've lost any desire to remain in the priesthood. **A male priest in The Episcopal Church.**

God challenged Moses to go to the Pharaoh. Moses immediately had an identity crisis. "Who Am I?" Moses knew he had no authority, skill or status. He was but a mere shepherd. He was a murderer. Moses knew he was a sinner - imperfect. How could he speak to anyone on God's behalf? Where would he get his authority to do so? God responded by reminding him, *"I will be with you"*.

The attacks on the clergy that I've reviewed go to the heart of their identity. Their credibility is brought into question. The attacks are on the very characteristics a pastor needs to speak with authority and power for God. They are designed to cast doubt on the pastor's honesty, truthfulness, spirituality and character. The hallmarks of the pastor's trustworthiness are put under the microscope. The clear intent is to cast a dark shadow.

It is a tactic that is as old as the human race. When the evidence cannot be attacked then the attack is on the person's credibility. The ultimate goal is to destroy the pastor's identity and integrity. The goal is to have their résumé stamped, *"unfit for ministry"*.

Persecutors of victims practice a form of moral exclusion. They begin by subjecting their victim to a different set of moral values, rules and sense of fairness than they extend to those in their own inner circle. This increases their ability to find their subject guilty of some nebulous sin that will leave them unacceptable.

The pain that a victim of sheep attacks experiences is complex. They will have multiple emotions. A pastor that has been driven to resign from a parish will be devastated. One of the most devastating of those emotions is the feeling that their identity and integrity have been maligned. The very backbone of their authority to be a pastor and priest has been splintered. Many face a crisis of professional and vocational identity. They question if they should continue in parish ministry or if they even want to. They begin to ask themselves, as did Moses, *"Who Am I to speak for God?"*

The Pain Is Real

The range of emotions will move from shock to sadness. Here is a representative sampling of the feelings some of these abused pastors shared with me for publication. My purpose in doing so is to validate the feelings and emotions of those that have suffered at the hands of antagonists. I am not aware of any forum within the greater Church that provides an opportunity to do so. It is my hope that sharing what others have endured can assist with the healing of even more victims. Your feelings are real. You are not having a pity party. You are not alone.

Betrayal. *"I thought that the people that attacked me were my friends."* That sentiment was expressed numerous times. The pastors felt betrayed by people they had considered to be friends and supporters. Trust became a major issue for them. During the attacks they had a difficult time even trusting those that wanted to help. Learning to trust again will prove a challenge to the abused pastor. This quote by Friedrich Nietzsche may summarize an abused pastor's trust issues, *"I'm not upset that you lied to me, I'm upset that from now on I can't believe you."*

Dismay. A Southern Baptist pastor told me, *"That congregation was dying. During my time with them we tripled the membership. Other pastors were calling me for advice. Then a small handful started some vicious rumors. Their intimidation was so intense I fear members of the congregation began to have doubts about me. I wanted it all to stop. The only way I believed I could do that was to resign. The good I was able to do for that congregation has been forgotten. Their nasty rumors are my legacy."*

Regret was frequently mentioned. Pastors accept a call to a new congregation because they think they can make a positive difference. They've prayed about it. They've asked their superiors for counsel and advice. They often discuss the possibility with their peers in ministry. They've considered their family's thoughts and feelings about a move to a new parish. Every pastor who has a first Sunday in a congregation knows that one day they will have their last Sunday in that parish. They hope their last Sunday will be a celebration of their ministry accomplishments with the congregation. A sheep attack negates that possibility. Attacked clergy often regret ever going to a particular congregation. They blame themselves for making what they reason should have been an obvious mistake. Their legacy is left in the hands of the very ones that set out to destroy them.

"You've got to help me understand this one." An Episcopal priest wrote me. *"The junior warden that orchestrated the attack on me got elected as the senior warden. He was then elected to chair our deputation to the General Convention. The man is a snake. I am so angry."* It was reported that antagonists often sought powerful positions of leadership after bullying a pastor into leaving.

"You positively will not believe this!" An exasperated Episcopal priest telephoned me. *"There was this woman that said some of the most vile things about me. The bishop has appointed her to serve as chaplain to the search committee for my replacement. Can you believe that? The woman accused me of every evil under the sun and the bishop made her the chaplain. I give up."*

Anger is a necessary part of the grief process. Attacked clergy will find themselves moving through each stage of that process. When the congregation or leadership bestows their blessing on those who have abused the pastor it does feel like insult has been added to injury. The anger in the injured pastor will multiply.

"There was this retired senior pastor who orchestrated the attack on me. I wasn't the first pastor that he'd targeted. He never got over the fact that they had never called him to be the senior pastor. Like the senior pastors before me I'm gone, but he's still there. What really burns me is that his band of followers is organizing an appreciation dinner for him and they are funding it out of the parish budget. Go figure." **A male pastor in The Lutheran Church Missouri Synod.**

Disappointment. *"Step by step they have dismantled every program and change I put into place."* A Methodist pastor reported. *"It's as though they are trying to erase all we accomplished from their history."* After an abused pastor leaves there will be a decrease in attendance and financial giving. With fewer resources many congregations will enter the survival mode. It is routine for the leadership to cut back on the number of Sunday services. This is often done in an effort to make the church appear more full. Any program that carried a financial cost will most likely be curtailed or eliminated. The abused pastor will feel that all their work has been in vain.

"I can't even think about going to another church." An abused Presbyterian pastor told me. *"I don't think my wife will ever darken the door of any church for as long as she lives."* **Disillusioned.** All the ideals that led a pastor and their spouse into full time

parish ministry are often smashed by a sheep attack. I spoke with abused pastor after pastor of all denominations that have not been present in any house of worship for months and some for years. Others attend so infrequently that their very presence in the congregation is seldom acknowledged. They describe themselves as spiritually numb. The enthusiasm they once had for the Church and for ministry is gone. Worship no longer inspires them. The activities of the Church are of no interest. As one Episcopal priest told me, *"I find reading the Sunday newspaper over a cup of Starbucks a lot more appealing. That's my new Church."*

Perhaps this pastor best expressed this lack of emotion. *"When I think about my former parish I don't feel anything. I'm not angry, but I don't feel happy either. I know there were some good times and we did some good things. What they did to my family and me really hurt. It took me a while to recover from the nasty things those people said and did. Now I just don't feel anything about my ministry in that place. I'm completely devoid of emotion when I think about it. I guess that means they no longer have any power over me."*

Rejection. *"I've gone through four search processes. As soon as they hear about my last experience I get that letter. You know the one. I gave my life to this Church. Now I have been ostracized."* That statement or one similar to it was frequently reported to me. Other clergy stated that their bishops and/or denominational authority had promised to help them find a new position but nothing ever happened. *"It's as though I have become an untouchable."* An Episcopal priest told me. *"No parish wants anything to do with me. I don't get it. I did nothing wrong. Yet a couple of sick people in my last parish have completely destroyed my ministry with their lies."*

These are but a few of the emotions that an abused pastor will experience. Their rollercoaster of feelings will not be limited to the ones listed above. Many of the pastors I heard from also suffered with the same emotions as those that have been sexually or physically abused. They were ashamed. They were embarrassed and humiliated. A sense of guilt and failure often haunted them even though they had done nothing wrong. Some even wanted to make excuses for the behavior of those that abused them. They wanted to minimize their own pain by rationalizing the behavior of their bullies. Like those in abusive sexual and physical relationships the pastors believed they could not control the situation. They were filled with fear and anxiety. They literally didn't know what they'd done wrong or how to make the situation better. None of their education or training had prepared them for the attack.

The pastors who resigned their parishes following an attack felt both a sense of sadness and relief. Most hoped and prayed that they were finished with the people who had bullied, attacked, slandered and abused them. Sadly, too many clergy discovered that these same antagonists would continue to try to destroy their character and any new ministry or career they assumed. Some even continue to defame their pastor into their retirement years.

At first I tried to reach out to them. I wanted to find a way that I could please them. I was so embarrassed. After only a few weeks I realized that my effectiveness in the congregation was being compromised. Others were beginning to believe what they were saying about me even though their accusations were completely without merit. They held their wealth and social standing in the parish over me and any person who dared to challenge them. I knew I needed to leave. At first it hurt. Now I just feel sad. **A female priest in The Episcopal Church.**

Where does a wounded pastor go for healing? Denominational executives promise to help. Multiple pastors reported that the promises were not kept. *"My bishop wanted me to go for a psychiatric examination. That really hurt. Four ego driven men attacked me, destroyed the parish and put my family through hell. And he has ordered me to get a psychiatric evaluation (?)."*

It was frequently reported that their clergy peers were too quick to believe the spin of the antagonists. They could not turn to them. Still others attended interim ministry training conferences. They met and were comforted by clergy that had suffered the same trauma. One pastor reported that those in attendance at his interim ministry training referred to themselves as "broken toys" as in the movie, *The Christmas Story*.

The Church, for the abused pastor, is no longer a place of healing. Attending worship only brings up the pain they've endured. They discovered that secular counselors, unfamiliar with the phenomenon, often sat in disbelief as the pastor opened their grief to them. A sheep attack is frequently unchartered territory even for mental health professionals.

Healing Begins

Healing begins by recognizing that you are not alone. At the rate of ten pastors an hour an ordained man or woman chooses to resign their parish and often their ministry. Lay professionals, lay leaders, and faithful Church members share in the collateral damage from a system that allows a pastor to be bullied and abused.

Healing begins by hearing a few of their stories as they reveal them in this book. Healing begins as one by one victims of sheep attacks accept that the abuse they endured is not information about them. So where does the abused pastor, church professional or faithful lay leader go for healing? How can they be made whole again? Will the Church ever be anything but a source of anxiety and bad memories for them? Those are some of the questions this book is designed to explore. The answers are critical components in the healing process.

I am so embarrassed. I know that the things that they are saying about me are false. It is as though I am paralyzed. I can't think clearly. I don't know how to counter their lies. Every bone and muscle in my body aches. I feel helpless. I talk with my psychologist but she just sits there. If I stop going to see her where do I go? I can't sleep. I can't eat. I feel empty and nauseous. My wife says that I need to get some help, but where? My bishop won't even return my telephone calls. Soon our money will run out. I've put my name in several search processes but it could be a year or more before they call anyone. Those four men have been so malicious I fear I will not be able to get another parish. I am filled with fear. I have a family depending on me but I have no job. What am I supposed to do? How does anyone get through this? I regret ever becoming a priest. I hate this. Please help. **A male priest in The Episcopal Church.**

For Reflection And Discussion

- The chances are that most every person will "lose" at least one job in their life. How is a "sheep attack" on a pastor different from any other job loss?

- Why would a person that a pastor felt was their friend and advocate cooperate with the antagonists?

- It was reported that abused pastors often share the same feelings of shame and embarrassment as those that have been physically or sexually abused. What factors contribute to those feelings?

- What would you say to an abused pastor to begin them on the path to healing?

"Anyone who welcomes you welcomes me, and anyone who welcomes me welcomes the one who sent me."
Matthew 10:40

Chapter 2

Wounded Lay Professionals

For thirty-one of my fifty-eight years, I worked as church secretary, a professional church musician and I presently serve as a church administrator. Four years ago I was hospitalized and treated for post traumatic stress disorder after nightmarish experiences in two consecutive churches over the course of thirteen years. When I read your email, which mentioned music directors, I wanted to add my voice to the many whom I call "the walking wounded". I had secular jobs in my career as well. But I have never encountered the underhandedness and meanness that I have seen in churches. Raising awareness among the clergy, vestries and congregations of antagonists and the ways they operate is necessary to address this cancer in the Church." **A female Church Administrator in The Episcopal Church.**

I first became aware that sheep attacks were not restricted to clergy when a musician friend of mine called my attention to a review of my book in a Roman Catholic Magazine. The review was published on June 5, 2010 in a magazine entitled, *Novus Motus Liturgicus or New Liturgical Movement*

In reviewing my book, Jeffrey Tucker, the sacred music editor, made the following observations.

"New personnel, new priests, and new pastors are not nearly as aware of the legacy of factional divisions as existing parishioners tend to be. I recall one occasion where a director of music dismissed the instructions of an idealistic new pastor on grounds that 'these guys come and go but the musicians stay'. He figured that he would outlast the pastor, and there was every reason to think that he was right. Directors of education and volunteers in various ministerial sectors believe the same thing.
Sometimes this can be explosive and lead to great tragedies, even to the point where new pastors and music directors are driven out of parishes. The force instigating the upheaval might be a small cadre within the parish. They probably do not represent the views of the majority. Nonetheless, they can be effective because they are well organized and know the lay of the land better than their opponents."

Mister Tucker gave the following example in the Roman Catholic Church.
.
A musician friend of mine arrived at a congregation and made wonderful changes in the music program. The choir was suddenly

large. It had previously been nonexistent. His program was praised in the national press. Parishioners were thrilled. Every Sunday was glorious and getting better. He put in some sixty plus hours per week in what was the most fulfilling job of his life. Again, he did not know that a tiny faction had targeted him at the outset. The innuendos started and he couldn't figure out their source. Many sleepless nights were the result. Within a matter of a single month, he was out the door. Again, he was completely blindsided by events and spent the next months puzzling about what happened. The music program fell apart." **Jeffrey Tucker, in a review of *"When Sheep Attack"* published in the publication *New Liturgical Movement.***

What has become apparent is that a congregational system that allows the senior pastor to be attacked will unleash the same behavior on other staff members. Two stories that were particularly demonstrative were called to my attention. A small group in a congregation that was known for targeting their senior pastors targeted a gifted musician with a national reputation. They wanted more *"Praise Music"* in the primary worship services. This classically trained musician tried to comply with their requests but failed to do so with the anticipated enthusiasm. The small group of antagonists was able force him into retirement. They then added insult to injury.

They orchestrated his retirement dinner at a private club, but limited the number of guests he could invite. He was not able to include his entire choir or even some of his family members that had driven hundreds of miles for the event. The parish vestry authorized that a retirement purse be collected for him. The many people that loved him and his music were quite generous with their donations. Then came the ultimate insult. The antagonists took the cost of his farewell dinner out of his retirement purse!

In another instance a couple of men on the governing board of the parish targeted the organist/choirmaster because of his sexuality. The rumors that he was going to be fired came to him on Christmas Eve. He went to the proper parish authority and was told that it was true. The choir threatened to boycott the Christmas services. To his credit, he talked them into remaining for the congregation's sake. Those were his final services in that parish. He did negotiate a severance package. He did not believe he could prove the real reason for his dismissal.

Forty-one years ago it happened to me. At age twenty-two, upon graduation from college in 1963, I became the first organist-director at a new Presbyterian church. I went with the pastor and a physician who was a leader in the church up to the Moller factory to see the organ, which was to be installed in the soon-to-be completed church. Meanwhile, we were meeting upstairs above an auto body shop. The excellent, experienced pastor left to become an administrator at a denominational conference center, and a new pastor arrived. He said from the pulpit that he did not preach the gospel but he preached the implications of the gospel.

He and I did not get along that well, but I thought the choir was loyal. Turned out that one of the 'grand dames' of the choir, who was married to 'old money' in town got mad because I didn't ask her to sing a solo. She led the attack on me and pulled the new pastor into the fray.

I saw what was happening and quit. So yes, it can happen to you. **An organist and choirmaster in The Presbyterian Church.**

A friend was very kind to introduce me to 'When Sheep Attack' a few days ago. This book assuaged my distress over events of the last five years or so when it seemed I was losing tuning contracts for no discernable reason. I have tuned the gargantuan organ at one of the largest churches since before God was born, have never had complaints before, and suddenly you are called before the Board of Deacons, told in no uncertain terms how lousy your work is and summarily dismissed... And you drive home in a fog wondering what they hey just happened. You have just been successfully attacked and vanquished by what

Doctor Maynard terms 'The Antagonists'. I think that if you have anything to do with eleemosynary institutions in any capacity whatsoever, you will find that the $15.00 for "When Sheep Attack" may save your sanity, not to mention your self-esteem. Not to even think of your JOB!" **An organist in the Christian Science Church**

Other Church Professionals

Wow! After a decade of lay youth work and my first year of seminary, finally someone who tells it like it is! I'm reading your book, 'When Sheep Attack', and is it ever fantastic! It validates and explains so much of my experience. Wow! Wow! Wow! **A female youth minister in a non-denominational church.**

Music Ministers were not the only church professionals I heard from. Youth Ministers and Christian Education Coordinators also shared their experiences. Here are just a couple of them.

There were six of them that had been running "invitation only" meetings in their homes. They then ran as a slate for the vestry. They even had a campaign slogan, "Elect us and the rector will be gone before Easter". There were people at the parish meeting that had not been to church in years. I'm not sure some of them were members of our church, but they voted anyway. After they were elected the six of them harangued the rector at every vestry meeting. Their innuendos so dominated the meetings that little else could be accomplished. All of us on the staff were aware of their unending phone calls to the rector, emails and unscheduled visits to his office.

We all knew that there was a retired priest in the congregation that had never gone to seminary pushing them to get rid of our rector. The rector accepted a call to another parish in a neighboring diocese. After he left the wardens brought each staff member that had been loyal to the rector before the vestry. The senior warden yelled at me and told me the vestry could no longer trust me to direct the children's choirs. There were people on the vestry that I considered friends that just sat there. They didn't even make eye contact with me. They said nothing in my defense. I was fired on the spot, as was every staff member that had spoken up for the rector. The hardest part was the retired priest was at the meeting as well. He just sat there and glared at each one of us with this twisted smile on his face. His eyes were shooting daggers at me. I never before believed in the existence of demonic spirits. I do now! **A children's choir director in The Episcopal Church**

Thank you for writing 'When Sheep Attack'. It described a similar experience I encountered. I was the Christian Education Coordinator for Children and Youth. The individuals described and their comments leapt off the pages. Your book has helped me so much during this healing process. While I have left the position as 'that small group' attacked my husband and me, the triangulation continues. **A female Christian Education Coordinator in The Episcopal Church**

The attacks leveled against lay ministers and other church professionals by a handful of antagonists only reinforce the observation that the problem is a systemic one. There is a dysfunction in the congregational system that allows just three or four people to bully any of the sacred ministers into leaving. The lay professionals in the situations I was able to document were leading successful programs. Their programs were growing. Their ministries were making a positive contribution to the life of the parish. The matriarchs and patriarchs appeared to be unwilling to stop the abuse. Obviously in some of the situations the abusers were the matriarchs and patriarchs.

All the elements that contribute to a successful sheep attack on a senior pastor are present. The essential staff catalyst was also present. In the case of music ministers it is often an influential member of the choir. As in the case of senior pastors, those that betray other members of the staff have garnered a small following and sufficient power to do their work. Again, like those who betray the senior pastor, the catalyst can be an active or retired member of the clergy or even a professional volunteer in the parish. The bottom line is that a congregational system that will allow the one percent to attack the senior pastor will allow that same or another one percent to attack any of their other sacred ministers.

Healing Begins

Accepting this singular fact will start the healing process for music ministers and any other lay professional. The nightmare that they unleashed on you is not information about you. It is information about the professional or voluntary staff member that chaplained the antagonists. It is information about the one or two percent of the congregation that abused you.

All the emotions of abused senior pastors will be yours. Healing begins by understanding that you are not alone. The prescriptive tools described in this book that have brought healing to others can bring healing to you.

For Reflection and Discussion

- Does it surprise you to learn that dysfunctional systems can target music ministers? Lay professionals? Why or why not?

- Why do you think antagonists might target a lay professional?

- How do you respond to the group that made the retiring organist pay for his retirement dinner with the retirement gifts from the congregation?

- Do you know a music minister or lay professional that was targeted? Were their circumstances similar to the attacks on a pastor?

"You did not choose me, but I chose you and appointed you to go and bear fruit – fruit that will last."
John 15:16

Chapter 3

The Congregation Will Be Wounded

What I saw today was the tears coming from the men. I saw one of our members, who is dying, at 8 o'clock crying and Father N going down to him at the peace and the man crying in his arms. The young faithful usher who cried at the altar rail.

The 10 o'clock service had 260 people, which is a full house for us. At the peace the rector, his wife and children stood at the top of the steps and received a standing ovation. My husband said it lasted for 5 minutes. One of the antagonists was standing in the room next to the altar and was surprised by the number of men crying.

My husband said there were a few old people at the reception but mostly, it was younger families.

It was a long line of people patiently waiting to tell Father N how much he meant to them and shaking his hand.

The champagne was my idea and a FABULOUS one. It was a celebration of the man and his ministry.

Those of us that supported him against the antagonists spent more money on the reception than we EVER HAVE! $150 for flowers, champagne, caterer for some items, $150 cake! Lots of food, but so many people it *was gone! Father N had a flute of champagne in his hand but never got past 10 feet into the reception room because of the well wishers and those who wanted to hug him or shake his hand.*

We, including Father N, did not anticipate this kind of outpouring particularly since the announcement went out on Thursday. The senior warden, also an antagonist, had been dragging his feet on sending out the invitations. The congregation only had two days notice.

It was a good day for him and for me and those who love him so much.

BTW His sermon was FABULOUS!!!! Over the top in class and right on the mark. **A female vestry person in The Episcopal Church.**

The follow up to the above story is that the average Sunday attendance in that parish after only two months fell to eighty worshipers versus the over two hundred average before the rector resigned.

I've had enough church politics to last me a lifetime. I am through. I'm finished with all churches. No more. Enough is enough! **A former male vestry member in The Episcopal Church.**

The pain experienced by the pastor or lay professional will be shared by members of the congregation. Far too often lay people have walked away from the church after supporting their church professional through this nightmare. The accounts of clergy spouses who no longer want anything to do with the church even if their clergy spouse remains active are far more numerous than may be recognized. The children of clergy in numbers not yet measured permanently wash their hands of the Church that was once such an integral part of their childhood.

I just finished reading 'When Sheep Attack' and my church could very well be case study Number 26. Our antagonists not only attacked our rector in the church, but also demonized him in the media to further discredit his reputation. My husband served as Senior Warden, and he was subjected to the same name-calling and attacks. Sadly, my family and several other families have decided that we cannot stay in the toxic environment and will be finding a new church home. The scenario was just as you described it – a popular priest, a growing parish, a new leadership growing, a surge in stewardship, etc. etc. But above all, there has been an amazing spiritual growth that the antagonists were not involved in. My personal opinion is that Satan has played a role in all of this. While I know my family and my fellow parishioners will find our way through this, I worry so much about our bright and extremely talented priests. I no longer hear excitement and enthusiasm in their voices – I hear pain and disappointment. I am praying that the bullying will soon end and they can begin to heal. **A senior warden's wife in The Episcopal Church**

In the first book the case studies did not address the consequences that lay leaders that supported the pastor suffered. It is an aspect that at least needs to be brought into the conversation. Several clergy reported that the antagonists threatened those that supported them. The livelihoods of some were threatened to the point that they silenced their support. One lay leader who had been a vocal supporter of their rector told me, *"I have to live in this town with these people. I have to do business with them. This is my church and it will continue to be my church no matter who the rector is."*

They circled me at the coffee hour. It was like bullies on a schoolyard. The four of them questioned my loyalty to the Church. They accused me of placing the welfare of the rector over the best interests of the parish. I tried to tell them that forcing our rector to resign was not in the best interests of the parish. They walked away. The rector did resign. My family left along with a lot of others.

Your book is spot on. **A former male vestry member in The Episcopal Church.**

Even after the pastor had left I received reports of lay leaders being targeted by the antagonists. One senior warden was publicly accused by the antagonists at a congregational meeting of giving the retiring rector a million dollar buy out. The antagonists who were present continued to verbally abuse him to the point that he simply resigned on the spot and walked out of the meeting and that parish.

Another reported that they had to transfer to a different church because at parish gatherings the antagonists would seek them out and attack them. They were accused of conspiring with the resigned pastor. Another lay leader reported that he belonged to a civic club with some of the antagonists. Those same antagonists had so poisoned some of the other members against him that at club luncheons they would turn their backs on him when he approached them.

The "problems" in our church began about six months before our Rector was called to a new parish out of the state. A group of people in the church decided that they didn't like the direction the priest was taking the church and they began to have meetings about their concerns with everyone invited except the priest. My husband and I attended these meetings and took the church canons. We told the vestry members what they were doing was wrong.

The Vestry members for obvious reasons took great offense to our interfering in their business. I actually don't remember how many meetings they held but these meetings were very damaging to the church family, the rector and his family. Our rector accepted a call from another church and by the grace of God he and his family moved on.

I decided I would run for vestry election. I had enough friends to support me and I got elected. The first vestry meeting I attended the Senior Warden began bashing the rector (now living in another state). I asked if we could not do that and if we could move on to handling the business of the church. The Senior Warden told me that he would meet with me later to discuss what I had said.

We made a plan to meet at the church later in the week. My husband went with me and the Warden did not like that. The conversation got very ugly as I confronted him about the vestry meeting and he told me he would do and say what he wanted to.

At this point in our Church life we were assigned an Interim Priest. He supported the Senior Warden. We had a funeral service (really the one from the prayer book!) and "buried" our former Priest's ministry.

That week a church meeting was called to discuss my rebellion and me; anyone could attend that had any interest in the church.

When I got to the church hall that night the chairs were set up in a circle for the vestry, and outside of the circle were seats for the congregation and there was a chair in the middle of the circle for me. There were lots of people in the church that agreed with me and came to support me and there were some that just thought they were coming to a normal congregational meeting and there were some that supported the Interim and Senior Warden.

I refused to sit in the middle chair and the Senior Warden didn't know what to do with that, I think he would have liked to tie me up and "burn me at the chair". Really nothing was accomplished at that meeting except to shame me and make the people that had no clue what was going on very upset. I recall one young man crying and saying, "I didn't know people in churches acted like this".

We stayed a few more months but the damage to the church and me had taken its toll. Many people left. My husband and I left and went to a very large non-denominational church and "hid" for a year. We did nothing to get involved and eventually the Lord began to heal the wounds. **A former vestrywoman in The Episcopal Church**

The additional follow up to the above story is that congregation split yet one more time after she and her family left. After the parish split for a second time the senior warden left to join a Pentecostal Church. The vestrywoman wrote that there is now nothing left of what was once a promising and growing congregation but *"a few old people and a lifeless liturgy"*.

One of the saddest documented cases was the owner of a small restaurant that had been the *"go to place"* for members of the congregation, especially after church programs on Wednesday nights. The antagonists who attacked the rector had been some of his most faithful regulars. The restaurant owner had been very vocal in his support of the rector. The antagonists blackballed his restaurant after the rector resigned and actively worked to keep others from eating there. The owner lost his restaurant. A few months later he suffered a debilitating stroke.

The retribution directed at lay leaders who supported the pastor was not a part of the original study. This hardly qualifies as an extensive look. I did receive sufficient response on this subject as a result of that first book to at least note it. Clearly, many of the laypersons that supported the resigned pastor find themselves targets as well.

Your book really described our story. A dynamic rector took our stagnant parish and brought life to it. He was the best preacher we've ever had and one of the best I've ever heard. Our four Sunday services were routinely packed to overflowing. The festival services were standing room only. Then a group that was meeting with an elderly priest in our congregation began their attacks. That elderly "gentleman" had also taken one of our assistants under his wing. He too began to organize his supporters against Father N as did a couple of the women on the staff. Word began to spread through the congregation as to just what they were doing. The elderly priest was most unkind in his criticism of Father N. We had a contentious annual meeting at which they got several of their group elected to the vestry. Our rector chose to retire soon after. No one blamed him, but our parish is not the same. So many familiar faces left. We are down to two services. Our main service is only half full most Sundays. If it weren't for the choir program I'm not sure anyone would come. I understand that it's just a matter of time until the early service will be canceled.

My problem, along with many others that have remained, is that I have lost respect for the people that attacked Father N. One of them is a verger. She leads the procession down the aisle with a smile of victory on her face. A few of them serve the chalice. My husband and I along with many others refuse to go to their side of the communion rail. I cannot accept the cup from them. We have an interim. He seems very kind. The group that attacked our rector has surrounded him like he is a long lost family member. Now that is downright confusing. The enthusiasm in our congregation is gone. We are hanging on *because we have a few friends still here, but all of us are visiting other congregations. We have adopted a "pay and pray" mode although our contributions now are miniscule to what we used to give the parish. I just don't see how our congregation will ever be the same.* **A lay woman in The Episcopal Church**

After experiencing the trauma of a sheep attack the parish will be wounded. It will be wounded because a parish is a community of people. The people who loved and supported the pastor have been hurt. One laywoman described it, *"I just feel so betrayed."* Another wrote me, *"I feel like our side lost."* A vestryman told me, *"I am so disgusted with that group. I can't even look at them. I've got to find another parish."* A Baptist minister told me that he'd been overwhelmed with the need to counsel and comfort the hurting members of the neighboring Episcopal Church. *"They're grieving over what happened to their priest. It's more than just grief. They are angry but don't feel like they have an arena in which they can express it."*

It also needs to be recognized that watching a pastor or lay professional being bullied and attacked may open old wounds for some of the members of the congregation. If in their own lives they have been bullied the memory of that pain will be resurrected. Those most dramatically affected will be those who were the victims of verbal, sexual or physical abuse. It is not unusual for members of the congregation to have to seek out a counselor for assistance after a sheep attack.

I have not been able to find a single congregation that failed to suffer negative numerical repercussions because of a sheep attack. In every scenario that negative impact was felt immediately. Attendance and giving both declined. Any growth the parish was experiencing was reversed. The leadership often tried to disguise the empty pews by decreasing the number of Sunday services. As reported in *When Sheep Attack,* on average, 28% of the active worshippers leave for another parish. 19% simply cease to attend worship in any congregation. Only one third continued to maintain their contributions at the current level. Up to 40% of the regular giving units will decrease their contributions and their participation in parish activities. If the rector has raised up and trained new leadership in the congregation my studies indicate that many of those will now leave the parish. I also discovered that often up to one half of the elected board will not only resign but also leave the parish.

I know what they did. Every member down at that church knows what they did. All their smirks and smug looks of condescension don't change a thing. Our rector was loved by ninety-eight percent of the people and that's not an exaggeration. He was one hell of a preacher - tears and laughter in every sermon. We were packed to overflowing almost every Sunday. I was an usher and we had to set up folding chairs down the side aisles most every service. It is unconscionable what they are saying about him. They can try to justify their actions but they can't hide the truth. We all saw what they were doing and those of us on the vestry could see right through them. Even if their accusations contained a grain of truth it's not enough to justify running him out like some sort of criminal. Our last Sunday there one of the hypocrites was sitting behind us. He tried to pass the peace with us. It was more than we could stand. My wife and I left. We will never go back to that church. As of this moment I'm not sure we will ever return to any church. **A male former member of the vestry in an Episcopal Church.**

Congregational Denial

"Our pastor has moved on. Everything worked out for the best. He's happy now. It was a terrible time, but we all survived. We did the right thing." After an attack many in the congregation will need to justify, even rationalize their behavior. They will need to paint a rosy picture for their own peace of mind. Their need to do so will depend on the degree to which they actively supported the pastor. In some cases it will be to justify their silence. Such rewriting of history needs to be

recognized for exactly what it is. There will be a need for some to deny the pain that their action or inaction brought to their pastor and their family. All the effort to paint a pretty picture does not gloss over the ugliness of the attack.

"I am now supposed to be happy about all this so that I can absolve them of their guilt. Some of the people who supported me have decided to stay in the parish. It's clear they don't want to feel guilty for doing so. They need me to be happy. The sickest comment one of them made to me was, 'I know it was just awful for you, but it was all a part of God's plan. Everything will work out for the best.' Screw that! Three people organized the movement to chase me out of that church. The only thing I am happy about is that they didn't use a rail with tar and feathers. I will be happy, but they're going to have to live with their guilt." **A male pastor in the United Methodist Church.**

Even bishops and denominational officers will want to rationalize the event. In reality they are denying something that happened on their watch they thought unthinkable. They have let down one of the clergy and many faithful members who had been given into their care. A very small group of antagonists had pressured them to hand over one of their own pastors for torment. So they, like many of the lay leaders in the congregation, must be able to justify it all. A rational explanation has to be given to quiet their conscience. Most often it comes at the expense of the targeted pastor. It is not unusual for them to explain the event as *"an unfortunate situation. The pastor got caught up in something that they could not control"*. One bishop described it as *"a tension that had been building between the rector and leaders in the congregation for some time"*. Another rector told me his bishop wrote the congregation and described the attack as *"a disagreement over the use of funds for parish priorities"*. I discovered that the most frequent explanation that was offered by bishops and denominational executives was *"the pastor got on the wrong side of some influential people"*. Having now reviewed the attacks in over two hundred congregations only one word comes to mind – **balderdash!**

  The pastors, lay professionals and lay leaders were bullied, intimidated, threatened, emotionally abused and blackmailed by a small handful of mean spirited people. Consistently the abusers represented less than two percent of the active membership in the parish. More often than not their antagonists were on the fringe of the congregation. Their participation was minimal and their financial support of the congregation miniscule to non-existent. There was no situation that spun out of hand. There was no disagreement over priorities. A small group of dysfunctional personalities targeted successful pastors and lay leaders for removal. The parallel to Good Friday is undeniable. Simply trying to rationalize this fact does not change reality. It also begs the question; just how long will those that did nothing be able to quiet their consciences?

Healing Begins

Healing begins for the lay leaders who stood by their pastor in the same way that it begins for their pastor. The attack on you is not information about you. It is information about the handful of ringleaders who organized the battle. It is information about the active or retired clergy person, staff member, or lay volunteer that served as their chaplain. All the prescriptive elements in this book are also for you.

Healing begins by recognizing that you did the right thing. You were blessed with an incredible "manure detector" that allowed you to see exactly what was happening. You have been blessed with a perceptive intelligence that allows you to distinguish lies from truth. Your intuition is highly developed and you were able to separate fact from fiction.

Your healing can begin by taking comfort in the following words by The Reverend Doctor Martin Luther King. *"Cowardice asks the question, 'Is it safe?' Expediency asks the question, 'Is it politic?' Vanity asks the question, 'Is it popular?' But, conscience asks the question, 'Is it right?' And there comes the time when one must take a position that is neither safe, nor politic, nor popular, but one must take it because one's conscience tells one that it is right."*

You are wounded because you did the right thing!

For Reflection And Discussion

- Share the stories of people you know that once were faithful members of a congregation but have walked away because of a sheep attack.

- Respond to the statement, *"Satan played a role in all of this"*.

- Why do you think the antagonists need to attack the lay leaders who supported the pastor even after the pastor has left the parish?

- Describe any congregation that to your knowledge increased membership and attendance following a sheep attack.

Don't just pretend to love others. Really love them. Hate what is wrong. Hold tightly to what is good. Love each other with genuine affection, and take delight in honoring each other.
Romans 12:10

Chapter 4

Healing A Broken Parish

Our downtown parish has been averaging 250 in worship on Sunday at three services. My last Sunday over 300 people attended. Since my "removal" I am told the average attendance is now 110. 20 of them are in the paid choir. The interim has now scheduled only one service on Sunday mornings. The impact on attendance you described in your book has been validated in that parish. I am also told that five of the vestry have resigned and transferred to another parish. **A male Episcopal Priest in The Episcopal Church.**

Bishops and denominational executives are often at a loss as to the best way to pastor the broken parish. The pattern most often utilized includes the following. The bishop or another denominational leader will hold a "listening" forum. Patiently they will listen to the outpouring of grief and anger. These listening forums can often be conflicted. Those who are happy the pastor is gone will try to put a better picture on the situation. They will reiterate their "accusations" against the pastor. Those comments are often followed by the rallying call for everyone to come together now and look to the future. The depth of the pain and grief of those who supported the pastor is too often underestimated. The antagonist's efforts to "spin" the reasons for the pastor's leaving only enhance their anger even more. These "listening" forums are often followed by a healing service. Those that feel the loss of their pastor will find little comfort. Those that "won" will often be observed congratulating themselves.

An interim pastor will then be appointed or selected. It appears that the antagonists were consistently appreciative and supportive of the interim and their ministry. The antagonists will wine and dine them, love them and praise their ministry. It's an excellent defense mechanism. In so doing the interim will be inclined to believe the spin that the pastor needed to go. They will report, *"There are no antagonists in this congregation."* It takes a very perceptive interim to see through their flattery. The result is that the dynamics in the system that allowed a sheep attack to occur are not addressed.

Too often, denominational executives believe that a long interim period will correct the situation. The interim period between pastors is often designed to allow the congregation to grieve and heal. A trained interim certainly can lead the congregation through that process. It can be a "time out" period from the anxiety and stress the congregation has experienced. As one woman told me, *"Peace has been restored to our Church, but there is no excitement. We are just treading water. We have lost so many valuable members. I don't think they'll come back."*

Honesty Critical For Healing

If systems theory is to be taken seriously, then simply restoring peace to the congregation is not enough. The healing moment for the wounded members of the congregation will come when the real reason for the pastor's leaving is brought into the light. If the former pastor's leaving was the consequence of a sheep attack then the interim period must be used to bring that out of the shadows and into the open. It is not a secret! The denominational executive and the remaining lay leaders may try to pretend so. The antagonists will put their spin on it. Most every member of the congregation already knows otherwise.

For the congregation's own health and future the behavior needs to be named. Before healing can take place the members of the congregation must be allowed to openly talk about the attack. Corrections need to be put into place to impede the behavior from occurring again. There is wisdom in the statement *"we don't keep secrets, our secrets keep us"*.

I discovered multiple congregations that went through the formulaic steps to healing. There was the listening session; the healing liturgy and the loving interim was employed. The real problem, however, was never brought into the conversation. The end story was that the antagonists were free to point to the named sin or failing of the senior pastor. The spin of the antagonists only deepens the anger in the congregation. Resentment will build among those members that desperately want the truth to be brought into the open. The end result is that their alienation from the parish is made complete.

The real dysfunction that is common knowledge in the congregation (and often the surrounding community) is that the pastor was targeted, bullied and attacked. The following statement or one similar to it was repeated over and over again.

"Everyone knows that group went after her. They wanted to get rid of her. They would stop at nothing until they thought they could find something on her that would stick. We all know it, but everyone walks around as though that isn't what happened. We just whisper about what they did. I want to shout the truth! The parish is just back to business as usual. Only now we have a lot fewer folks on Sunday and the money has dried up." **An elder in The Presbyterian Church USA.**

Pretending that the systemic dysfunction does not exist will not correct it. It must be named and confronted. I also contend that openly naming and discussing what happened is a critical component in the healing process.

The hurting hearts of the injured members of the congregation need it. To do otherwise will only cause many faithful lay people wounded by the experience to leave. Far too many of them will permanently walk away from the Church sad, angry and disgusted. Some will stay but become passive to inactive members. Their bitterness toward the denominational authorities and the antagonists will accelerate. Others will seek a new congregation but will choose to become uninvolved. Many will never return to their former ministries of leadership in any parish. That is yet one more loss for the greater Church.

"When Sheep Attack" arrived this afternoon – I just finished reading the book. Very well written, a bit hard to read some parts; but not as hard as it would have been to read a year ago. AND if enough read it and take it seriously then the tools of spiritual warfare that you wrote about will not be so sharp! From my little corner of the world, something about seeing in print 'this is your life' is reassuring that I did all that I could do. I ordered six copies: one for my senior warden, one for my bishop, one for my canon to the ordinary, one for the priest who now serves my former congregation, one for another damaged priest from my Clergy Leadership Project class and one for me.

My former congregation is very damaged and still suffering. Nothing really has been resolved, merely muted, and they have now gone from a fulltime priest to a yoked ministry where they get one quarter of the new priest's time. I am now priest number two that left under similar circumstances, fourteen years apart. I have no proof, but I think one retired priest and a former part-time vicar offered coaching to the antagonistic group. The other retired priest, also a former part-time retired vicar, got caught in the plotting – a victim of his own poor hearing and efforts to try and calm 'the old guard'. The antagonists sensing they 'have won' no longer have the same drive or commitment to the life of the church, since they have gotten rid of me. The Bishop, the new yoking arrangement, team ministry, and new vicar are keeping a tight rein on them.

I received a moving call the other day from a member of my former church, one who was and always has been supportive of me. This person called to say how sorry he and his wife were for the damage that church did to my late husband and me. He also hoped the damage would not impede my ministry and good works, and how sorry he was that we went through all of that for so long.

Now, having been at this new church for almost a year, I am learning to trust people little by little again. The first six months, now being in a healthy place, I realized how sick the situation was where I had been before. A very supportive senior warden (and his family), vestry and congregation; all are gratefully appreciated. Twice this past year my senior warden has taken me by the shoulders and looked me in the eye and said, "Don't worry. I don't know what happened in your last parish, but it won't happen here."

The church is supposed to be the hospital, not the one that hurts. And yet, as long as we have people who believe it is 'un-Christian' to say 'no' to some people we will always have this element of the church to deal with and sadly (yet hopefully) learn lessons from these storms. **A female priest in The Episcopal Church**

The denominational leaders and the healthy leadership in the congregation must be honest before healing can occur. The senior minister was attacked by a handful of people. The current denominational executive and the members of the congregation either actively or passively allowed it to happen. Any other explanation is a smoke screen. The demon must first be named before it can be dealt with. The congregation must take an honest look at itself. The conversation at the healing workshops needs to be focused on the health of the congregation's system, not the supposed shortcomings of their previous senior pastor. Like a house silently destroyed from inside with dry rot, the parish will continue toward the same end. Those who want to spin the dark secret of the sheep attack may be able to successfully do so. The disease in the system, however, remains. Failure to name it and address it means that it's just a matter of time until another senior pastor in the parish will be subjected to the same nightmare.

The question that needs to be explored is whether or not this is asking too much of interim clergy? Many of the clergy that have entered interim ministry have already endured one or more sheep attacks themselves. They may not have the inner strength needed to confront the antagonists even in an interim situation. Interim clergy are further dependent on bishops and denominational executives to recommend them for their next assignment. If the interim has failed to restore peace to the congregation they may not get another job. So if we cannot ask the interim clergy to bring the dysfunction in the congregational system to the light - then who will be able to do so?

It was great talking to you. I am still thinking about the "recovery" issue for your new book. I can't wait to read it. I really stand by my view that a course on this subject should be required by the Archbishop for every bishop. By definition, they got there by not ending up in a difficult parish. It also got me to thinking about a question you posed a couple of years ago about what do interims do: If they take on the antagonists can they get another assignment? Bishops need to be trained on how to protect interim rectors and how to be an active part of finding their next assignment. Bishops should have to document that the assignment for the interim is in a "challenging" parish at the time the interim is recruited and that document could be given to the interim for future use. Maybe the Senior Warden could be given an easy to file document that can stay with the interim. The "Church" is declining fast enough on its own. It doesn't need unhealthy parishes to exacerbate the problem. **A male former Senior Warden in The Episcopal Church.**

Healing Begins

The wounded members of a congregation will share a common prescription with their wounded pastor or lay professional. They need to talk about what happened. If they remain silent their wounds will become gangrenous. Allowing the antagonists to continue to spin their story only increases their pain and anger. Their sense of justice demands that the antagonists be exposed for exactly what they did. Based on the experiences that form the foundation for these books, it is highly unlikely they will be offered such an opportunity in the congregation. Yet these truth tellers need to speak. Your healing begins by doing that very thing. Follow the scriptural admonition to speak the truth in love. Hearing yourself do so will contribute to your healing.

For Reflection and Discussion

- What methods would you use to "put a parish back together" following a sheep attack?

- Why do you think the antagonists often embrace an interim?

- Discuss this statement – *"We don't keep secrets. Our secrets keep us"*.

- What words of healing could you say to parish members wounded by a sheep attack? Do you think your words would help bring them back to the Church?

SECTION TWO

There Was Nothing More You Could Have Done

"When you enter a house, first say, 'Peace to this house.' If someone who promotes peace is there, your peace will rest on them; if not, it will return to you. Stay there, eating and drinking whatever they give you, for the worker deserves his wages."
Luke 10:5-12

Chapter 5

Controlling The Narrative

It is the most humiliating part of the entire nightmare. The people that attacked me continue to try to destroy me. Many in my former congregation now believe the lies they tell about me. I don't have any way to defend myself. Do I send a letter to the entire parish? Do I begin by telling them about the abusive telephone calls? The intimidation? Or should I open with the death threats they made against me? Is it acceptable to write my former parish and tell them that the things being said about me are a lie? How can any priest counter this ugliness? **A male priest in The Episcopal Church.**

Once the antagonists have gotten their way they find themselves in the horns of a dilemma. If their behavior has become public knowledge the healthy members of the parish will condemn them for it. On the other hand what good is a victory if you can't brag about it? So the antagonists must cover both bases. On the one hand they must be able to justify their behavior as righteous. They do that by further maligning the pastor. Once they've been able to completely denigrate the pastor, they then believe they can justifiably boast about *"getting rid of them"*. They not only make themselves look good, but they want to be seen as the 'saviors of the parish' deserving of big gold watches for their service. The fact that the parish itself goes into decline is unimportant. The fact that many members leave is irrelevant. Their primary concern is that they end up looking like the good guys. The only way that can happen is to completely destroy their pastor even after they leave.

The wardens, the bishop and I had all agreed on a letter to be mailed to the entire parish that would be a 'win win' for the antagonists, the parish, and me. They had created so much turmoil around my leaving the parish was angry and fragile.

The congregation was well aware of the antagonists and their activities. The bishop hoped the letter would calm the waters. All in all it was a good letter and most likely would have done just that. The letter was on my administrative assistant's computer and was to be mailed out the next day. I left the parish that same day to make arrangements for my move to a new position in another state.

The two wardens that were also leading the attacks on me broke into my assistant's office that night and changed the letter on her office computer. They did so in order to plant seeds of doubt about me and make themselves look like heroes. They had the letter in the mail to the entire parish before my assistant, the bishop or me were even aware of it. **A male priest in The Episcopal Church**

Antagonists see themselves as saving the parish from a pastor that could more accurately be labeled a reprobate. They are equally determined that their fellow parish members and all the folks in the greater community see things their way. In order to establish bragging rights they try to control the story. **They need to do so by making sure that their target does not have any opportunity for rebuttal.** As one senior warden told me, *"They knew they had to get something on her so they just kept digging until they could find something they thought would stick. Then they twisted it around and blew it all out of proportion. That handful was the only group that thought their accusations justified chasing her out of the congregation. Their plan didn't work. Most of us knew exactly what they had done. They had made the poor woman's life miserable. They had put together a smear campaign filled with lies and half-truths and they continue to spread their vile to this very day. I honestly don't know how she stood it as long as she did. We never believed their story. The spin doctors in Washington could learn a thing or two from those boys."*

The following story illustrates this point so well.

You would think that the weeks of intimidation, threats (including death threats) and promises to "get something on me that would stick whether true or not" would be enough for them. I received a call to another parish so I took it just to get away from them. My wife and I were so relieved to put those awful people in our rear view mirror.

The parish had become very aware of the antagonist's behavior. A great number of them even stormed the meeting of the vestry the week before I resigned. The antagonists and the four leaders in particular became targets of the congregation's anger when I announced I was leaving. They decided they needed to defend themselves against the wrath of the parish. They took advantage of my absence and decided to follow through on their threat "to get something on me". The former school board chairman, also one of the four ringleaders, pointed them to a transaction in the Rector's funds made four years before.

My contract of call with the parish specified that my children would attend the parish school with all costs being waived by the school. For the first ten years of my ministry the parish school honored that portion of the agreement. That same school board chairman had decided to change the policy regarding my children's fees and books. I began receiving statements from the school. I called this to the attention of my senior warden at the time.

He tried to have a discussion with the board chair about it, but he wouldn't relent. He told my senior warden that it was just a matter of time until the school gained its independence from the parish. After that the school would have no obligation to honor any portion of the Rector's Letter of Agreement.

My senior warden decided that it would be best not to put the vestry and the school board on a collision course. The tension was already approaching the explosive stage over separation. He decided to contact some of the members of the congregation that strongly supported my ministry. He asked them to make a directed donation so that I could use them to have the parish continue to honor the school's portion of my contract

The senior warden that had raised the funds had since died. I was now living over a thousand miles away and had no knowledge of what they were doing. I began receiving telephone calls from those that supported me in that parish. They advised me that my reputation, honesty, and character were being trashed. The wardens were telling people I had mismanaged my discretionary funds. I had become fodder for the town gossips.

Basically, the two wardens put me on trial before the parish leadership. It was a trial I knew nothing about. They waited until I was at a safe distance. They made certain that I would not be able to respond to their allegations. The end result for the parish was that those that had made the directed gifts left that parish along with hundreds of others. The antagonists had taken a perfectly legitimate transaction and twisted it to justify their behavior. Because they did not reveal the complete story about that one transaction they cast doubt in the congregation on my entire management of the rector's funds. I was never given the opportunity to respond or defend myself. **A male priest in The Episcopal Church**

I think one of the most revealing examples of an antagonist's need to control the story by smearing the former minister came to me at a book signing. A woman who had worked diligently to remove the senior minister of that congregation told me, *"You know he was mentally ill. He and his wife are both crazy. We wanted to give him a farewell reception using our silver service and all. He declined. Can you believe that? We were going to give him a nice reception utilizing our silver bowl and he wouldn't let us."* Now I ask you, dear reader, how is any pastor ever going to defend themself against such viciousness? This is especially true when they no longer live in the community and may reside hundreds or even thousands of miles away. Maybe George Costanza's famous line in the television series, *Seinfeld* summarizes it best, *"It's not a lie if you believe it."*

Clergy As Unknowing Co-Conspirators

Salt is added to the wounds when other members of the clergy are validating the slander! In response to *When Sheep Attack,* pastor after pastor reported that after they left they received virtually no support from the other clergy in their diocese, presbytery or conference. Their neighboring clergy not only chose to believe the gossip and rumors, but to repeat and embellish them. A Methodist pastor wrote me, *"Not a single pastor that I'd worked with in my conference telephoned me to ask what happened. None wanted to hear my side of the story."*

What really hurt was when I learned that some of my fellow priests that I'd considered to be my friends were repeating and even expanding on the stories the antagonists had created. Several of them knew the truth but chose to believe that where there is smoke there must have been fire. There was no smoke. There was nothing but a smoke screen. **A male priest in the Episcopal Church**

When other clergy repeat the rumors and gossip they become defacto mouthpieces for the antagonists. They become co-conspirators with dysfunctional personalities that sought to destroy the ministry of one of their sisters or brothers in Christ.

It needs to be stated again that once a clergy person leaves the community the antagonists will use every opportunity to control the story. Facts are of little assistance. Gossip fueled by the antagonists in an effort to look like the good guys that were in control of the situation from the start will dominate the final chapter. Seldom is the targeted pastor in a position to rebut the slander.

An Episcopal priest wrote, *"I couldn't believe it when I heard that a priest that I had considered my friend was telling people that I had been fired. We were in a small group together. He knew the entire story. I had told him just what the antagonists were doing to my wife and me. He even seemed sympathetic and supportive in the group. Then it came back to me. He was telling people I had been fired. I had told him how my wife was begging me to get her away from those people. She could not stop crying. I told him about my health problems. I had to get away from those toxic people and he knew it! It was as if he was taking delight in trashing my reputation, my ministry and me. I thought he was my friend."*

A Methodist pastor wrote that he tried to tell a couple of his colleagues about the attack on his ministry. *"They just rolled their eyes at each other. That hurt more than what the bullies had said about me."*

Any clergy person that has only served healthy parishes is fortunate indeed. If the responses I've received to *When Sheep Attack* is any indication, however, these same clergy are a bit too anxious to believe that where there is smoke there must have been fire. The better response would be to follow the example of the former rector of a parish that telephoned his successor who had left. He asked, *"Tell me what happened? There are so many rumors and none of them reflect well on you. I want to know so I can help set the record straight."* All clergy could follow that man's example and seriously examine their consciences before becoming partners with the antagonists in their mission of destruction.

One closing word to the clergy who have been fortunate enough to never been targeted by a small group of antagonists. Up to now you are an exception, but don't believe for a second that it can't happen to you. None of the two hundred plus clergy in these books believed it would happen to them. It did! Perhaps this one closing story will serve to motivate all clergy to think twice before they become *instruments of the antagonists* instead of *instruments of peace*.

I spoke with the spouse of an Episcopal priest who had left his parish after being tortured by a small group. She was expressing her disappointment that the other clergy in the diocese were treating them like lepers. Most of them believed the horrible things that had been said about her husband. This is her story.

Two years ago we were called to pastor a new church after fifteen years of successful ministry in another diocese. My husband took two trips to interview and preach at the new church. A team from that church came and visited our parish incognito. We accepted the call. The installation was a three-day affair. Barely three months after we arrived the rumbling started. One disgruntled member was mad about the senior warden. They wanted my husband to get rid of him. Before we knew what was going on it became personal. The attacks were so vicious that the bishop encouraged my husband to resign. The bishop promised that we would be 'taken care of.' Even after we walked away they would not relent. A couple of months after my husband resigned he had a stroke following what had been continuous harassing phone calls from the disgruntled group.

Occasionally, someone will ask me what happened. When they do, I just give them a copy of your book. 'Read this.' I tell them. 'Then you'll know exactly what happened.' **A female spouse of a priest in The Episcopal Church.**

Clergy that have been abused are often reluctant to get in a shouting match with their former antagonists. It is difficult to correct accusations and rumors. They are even more difficult to correct when the former pastor is totally unaware that they even exist. Consistently antagonists prefer to sign their emails, notes and letters as *anonymous.* Once a pastor leaves a congregation they will be totally dependent on those that know the real story to correct the false accusations and rumors.

Healing Begins

This is one of the most difficult aspects of an attack. Healing begins by accepting that the narrative just may be beyond your control. It also begins by accepting that fact that those that believe the spin of the antagonists may actually want to do so. In other words, they were never your friends. To repeat an old adage, *"You never need to explain yourself to anyone. Your true friends don't require an explanation. And your enemies won't believe anything you say."*

Your healing begins with the knowledge that the overwhelming majority of the parish, perhaps as many as ninety percent or more, will refuse to believe anything the antagonists have to say. Your healing begins with the knowledge that there are truth tellers in the parish that will speak the truth. Your healing begins by leaving the antagonists and their narrative in the rearview mirror. You are now free to write your own narrative.

For Reflection And Discussion

- Do you agree with the author's findings that the antagonists need to control the final story so that they can "establish their bragging rights"? Why or why not?

- What do the antagonists have to gain by slandering a pastor years, even decades after they leave a parish?

- The antagonists forcefully work to control the story. Clergy subjected to a sheep attack often become unemployable in the Church. What do you think the Church can do to remedy this?

- Do you agree that the antagonist's spin surrounding a pastor's leaving gains credibility when other clergy repeat it? Why or why not?

"I will raise up for myself a faithful priest, who will do according to what is in my heart and mind. I will firmly establish his house, and he will minister before my anointed one always."
I Samuel 2:35

Chapter 6

The Antagonists' Preferred Target

Those people dared to call themselves Christians, but they gave no consideration to just how their actions would impact my family and me. I've always been a preacher. It's the only thing I know, but now I am without a pulpit. We had to move out of the church owned house. We are living with my wife's parents. We have no income and no health insurance. There were only three of them, but they destroyed my ministry. When I went to that parish it was dying. We'd just finished a new worship center. I did nothing to deserve this. **A male pastor in the Church of the Nazarene.**

For the antagonists, the success that the parish and the senior minister are enjoying most often serves as the 'final straw'. Growth in any organization destroys the balance of power. Those that have grown comfortable always being in control will have less. The most important people, or at least those that perceive themselves as such, will be less recognizable. The complaints in a successful organization escalate up Maslow's Chart of Hierarchical Needs. In a struggling parish the complaints surround basic survival needs.

> *"We need more members."*
> *"We need to attract young people."*
> *"We need to increase our stewardship."*
> *"We need a planned giving campaign."*
> *"Evangelism, that's what we need."*
> *"I remember when our Sunday School was full."*

When a parish is enjoying growth and success the complaints mirror the needs at the top of the chart.

> *"I don't know what's going on in this place."*
> *"We need better communication."*
> *"I didn't get a chance to greet the pastor last Sunday."*
> *"I just don't feel like anyone even knows my name."*
> *"There are so many new people I don't know any of them."*
> *"All these children and young people are wonderful, but so noisy."*

The "powerbrokers" in the congregation that believe they are in control are seldom willing to accept less control. They want more! If they are used to being the big fish in the small pond they will not be content to be a smaller fish in a bigger pond. To grow, a parish must be creative, even entrepreneurial.

This will demand that everyone in the system also change. Change is always resisted. Rare is the person who wants more of what they don't have. They want more of what they already have. The antagonists want more power, not less. They want more visibility, not less. They want to increase their importance, not diminish it.

Irresistible Clergy Targets

I now realize I did all the wrong things. I believed my conference superintendent and the leadership in the congregation. They said they wanted to grow. They wanted to attract young families and youth. Their youth program was non-existent, much of the space they had for Sunday School sat empty on Sunday mornings. They struggled each month to meet their obligations. After just four years we had an active and vital youth program, the Sunday School classrooms were all full, we were looking at ways to expand the nursery as young families filled our formerly empty pews on Sunday mornings. Not only had our stewardship giving increased, but we had put together an operating reserve fund to see us through the lean summer months. Then out of nowhere I was hammered by a small group of the old guard. Their assaults were directed at my character. They questioned my honesty and said I could not be trusted. There was so much more, but as you pointed out in 'When

Sheep Attack' it was brutal and exhausting.

I have since been assigned to a new congregation. The last one began to decline immediately. The youth program is once again non-existent, many of the Sunday School classrooms are now empty, and there is no longer a need to expand the nursery. The good news is that the old guard can now park in 'their spots' in the parking lot and sit in 'their pews'. There are no new people cramping their style.

Now that I am in my new assignment I am going to do things different. I am going to be an on-call chaplain for the important people. The word 'evangelism' is no longer in my vocabulary. I am not going to do anything to rock the boat. I will welcome new members if they choose to come but I am not going to do anything to encourage them. Along with the old guard I am just going to shake my head and wring my hands over our monthly finances. I have it figured that my new ministry plan will allow me to stay here until I choose to leave or retire. By then I will have achieved the level of 'beloved'. The parish will honor my ministry with them by hanging a large portrait of me in the entrance hall; name a building or the fellowship hall after me. Gosh, they may even put my likeness in a stained glass window. **A male pastor in The United Methodist Church**

I'd really like to think that the above letter was written tongue-in-cheek. For clergy that have successfully turned around a dying parish and then been attacked for doing so, it's easy to accept the pastor's cynicism. The problem with the letter is that most all clergy can see the truth it contains.

My studies indicate there is a type of clergy that antagonists find irresistible. They are the clergy that successfully turn around and build up dying or declining parishes. In the majority of the cases I've examined, the senior pastor or lay professional had turned around the congregation or the ministry program.

In order to accomplish a turnaround, new and entrepreneurial ideas were required. Dying or dead programs were buried. New leaders and leadership were recruited, raised up and given authority and power. In order to turn around a parish or a ministry program, the pastor or lay professional possesses certain personality characteristics that can contribute to success. Here are some of them that can be easily observed.

- Independent – they think for themselves. They are not easily swayed by flattery or intimidation.

- Self-actualized – they will have a strong sense of self. They know who they are. They understand their strengths and weaknesses.

They know how they are different from others and have accepted it.

- Slightly unorthodox – they do not fit into the mold that often frames those that enter the ministry.

- Entrepreneurial – creative clergy that often color outside the lines. They do so in order to accomplish their ministry objectives.

- Successful –in spite of resistance they have a record of successfully building up congregations and ministry programs.

- Knowledgeable – they have a history of trying to improve their skills through continuing education, reading and advanced degrees.

- Determined – people pleasing is simply not in their DNA. Being faithful to the demands of the Gospel is their guiding force.

Clearly, the above is not the profile for co-dependent clergy. These are not pastors willing to play the game the antagonists would demand. Simply contrasting the profile that these studies have painted of antagonists with this clergy profile could lead to the belief that the conflict is inevitable. But that only raises the question about the system at work in the congregation. Clearly, there are self-actualized clergy that are never attacked by antagonists. That is just further evidence that the attacks on successful clergy are not information about them. The dysfunction is in the congregational system. The parish is being held hostage by a system that allows the antagonists to act out.

Healing Begins

Your healing begins by acknowledging and accepting that you were true to yourself. You did not sell yourself into some sort of "bonded servitude". You refused to shuffle your feet and become the antagonist's "boy or girl". You most likely did exactly what the parish leaders asked you to do. You turned around a declining parish. The evidence is in the attendance and stewardship roster. You raised up new leaders. You brought vitality to a dying congregation. Those that resented your success organized the attack. Your healing begins with the realization that you did your job.

For Reflection and Discussion

- The evidence is that the work of the antagonists reverts a dynamic and growing parish into a stagnant or dying one. The pastor not only leaves the parish but up to forty percent of those attending before the attack will leave the church as well. Why don't you think the antagonists feel any remorse for the fruit of their work?

- Name some of the other things members give up when a congregation begins to grow.

- Respond to this statement. "There is a reason that small congregations choose to stay small."

- Describe your experience in a parish being led by an entrepreneurial senior pastor.

"Therefore confess your sins to each other and pray for each other so that you may be healed. The prayer of a righteous person is powerful and effective."
James 5:16

Chapter 7

No Apology - No Repentance

After reading "When Sheep Attack" last evening, I have to tell you that this is my story. I have been ordained sixteen years and ministered with some fine people in four congregations. My story happened in my last diocese when the former rector and his cohort, a retired priest who also remained in the congregation, did just what you described in the book. And the story was then carried to the former bishop of my present diocese. As a result, my career has been ruined. The one difference is that the parishes in which I serve are smaller than those that I think you are describing but the results are the same and the pain, isolation and disbelief are identical. And I, too, love the people called by God to be in this place and this time as I hope to finish out my years here but I have earned my stripes and will always be cautious. **A female priest in The Episcopal Church.**

Clearly, when a handful of people in a congregation seek to destroy a clergy person's ministry, that behavior does not correspond to the fruit of the Spirit described in Holy Scripture. Maturing Christians seek to grow in understanding, love, forgiveness and joy. The behavior of antagonists does not mirror those virtues.

A critical component in the faith journey is to routinely examine our thoughts, words, deeds and omissions for sin. In particular, the goal is to increase our sensitivity to just how our words, deeds and the things we have left undone impact the lives of others. Have we injured them? How have we failed them? Intentionally or unintentionally have we *"done those things that we should not have done and left undone those things that we should have done"*?

It appears inconceivable that anyone could week after week hear the readings from scripture, sing the words in the hymnal, be encouraged from the pulpit, offer the prayers of confession and not have their consciences stirred. In one of the cases I was told of a retired priest who had led sheep attacks on the previous three rectors. A new rector arrived and he immediately rallied his troops to do the same thing again. A couple of the strong leaders in the parish had grown weary of his shenanigans and confronted him. They told him as firmly as they could that what he had done and was attempting to do again was not only sinful; it was evil. He met their challenge with a smile and a twinkle in his eyes. He insisted that they needed to understand, *"I am doing God's work"*.

Classical Christian Spirituality teaches that there are four parts to repentance. It begins with the knowledge that one's words or actions are in fact sinful. That knowledge is followed by contrition. There is genuine sorrow in the person for what they have said or done. Contrition is followed by the need to confess. If possible confessing to the person that has been injured. The fourth part of the repentance process is the determination to change one's life so as to not fall temptation to that sin again.

Antagonists appear to be incapable of any of these steps. They adamantly deny that their words and actions are sinful. To the contrary they brag about what they have done. *"We fired her!"* *"We exposed that so-called preacher."* They have no contrition for their deeds and if given the opportunity will repeat them. Instead of amending their lives they continue to try to destroy their victim even after they believe they have won the battle.

Once again the obvious needs to be pointed out. I have not been able to find even one case where the antagonists that bullied a clergy person have repented! Characteristic of this behavior is the absolute inability to accept responsibility for the damage and pain they have brought not only into the lives of the clergy, but to their parish and the people in it. One cannot help but ask how can they be so blind to the misery their actions bring to others? This indisputable fact needs to be repeated once again. I have not been able to document a single case where the antagonists have apologized or asked forgiveness.

I did discover cases where one of the antagonists would pretend to be repentant. Whether motivated by an alcohol induced stupor or peer pressure they uttered vague words of repentance, but never to their victim.

The following is a perfect illustration.

I still have not returned to a church and have no plans to do so. I left St. N's over two years ago. The antagonists (as you call them) executed their campaign against me with military precision. Not so surprising since two of them are retired military officers.

The week after I left the Bishop held a congregational meeting. The leader of that group gave the most unbelievable speech. He was even able to conjure up some tears. He said, "It all just got out of hand. This wasn't what I wanted. I was just trying to help Father N be a better rector." I wasn't there but evidently he won some folks over and some of my supporters were seen hugging him.

He went home immediately after the meeting and sent an email to the group that had attacked us. In it he thanked all of them for their help in removing me and in true military style ended the email with the words - "mission accomplished!" He failed to edit his mailing list. He included the members of the vestry. Many of them had supported me. A couple of the vestry forwarded a copy of the email to me. They included copies of emails from his group congratulating him on his leadership and a "job well done". I am so glad that I chose to get out of that sick place. **A male priest in The Episcopal Church.**

The antagonists deny their victims one of the most important ingredients they need for their healing. Every victim of abuse craves to hear those that abused them apologize. Before an abuser can apologize, however, they must first accept that what they have done was wrong. In spiritual terms they have to repent. The words *"I am sorry"* are some of the most healing words any abused person can hear. Not a single one of the clergy, church professionals, or lay leaders I interviewed has heard those words from their abusers.

To the contrary, they continue to spread their vindictiveness against their target years and even decades after they have gotten their way. Having destroyed their target's ministry in one parish they often go to great lengths to continue to try to destroy their ministries in any future parish they attempt to serve. The antagonists possess a level of viciousness that simply cannot be attributed to a spiritually healthy personality that accepts responsibility for their own wrongdoing. They appear to be completely insensitive to any but their own feelings.

Researcher Tyler G. Okimoto at the University of Queensland in Australia has made some interesting observations. His research on this subject concludes that when a person refuses to apologize they actually feel more empowered. As long as a person does not come to terms with their wrongdoing they maintain a position of superiority over their victim. Their sense of self-worth actually increases. His research uncovered an even more surprising observation. People that refuse to apologize have their feelings of integrity boosted. Okimoto suggests that his research refutes the notion that apologizing will actually make a person feel better in the long run. His work is certainly applicable to understanding the behavior of antagonists.

One of the prerequisites to an apology is to be able to empathize with the pain inflicted on a victim. Closely related to that empathy is the desire to reconcile with them so that a harmonious relationship can be restored and continued. In each of the experiences that I've documented, the antagonists appear to be insensitive, even impervious, to the pain they have inflicted. The evidence is that they will continue to unleash their abuse even after achieving their objective. It can also be clearly shown that the antagonists make no effort to reconcile with their victims.

One can easily surmise that they want nothing but a hostile relationship with those they target. Applying Okimoto's research to their behavior leads to an apparent conclusion. By continuing to degrade their pastor victims and refusing to apologize, the antagonists actually increase their feelings of power and self-worth.

Healing Begins

Healing begins by accepting the following about antagonists. The defense mechanisms of projection, rationalization and justification are fully developed in their personality wiring. These defense mechanisms are utilized to keep them from having to come to terms with the consequences of their own behavior. By projecting their own dark sides on their targets their feelings of superiority are enhanced even further. They are then able to justify sitting as judge, jury and executioner on their own pastors.

Your healing begins by not anticipating that your antagonists will ever apologize. They will never accept responsibility for their behavior. They have chosen to believe their own spin. If there is a lesson to be learned it may have been best summarized by Maya Angelou. *"The first time someone shows you who they are, **believe them**."*

For Reflection And Discussion

- Is it possible that the antagonists are completely blind to the hurt and pain their actions are inflicting on the pastor and the parish? Agree or disagree and explain.

- Why does an apology from their abusers bring healing to the victims?

- Do you know of a situation where the antagonists apologized for their behavior?

- Respond to the words by Maya Angelou, *"The first time someone shows you who they are, believe them."*

"Two men went up into the temple to pray, one a Pharisee and the other a tax collector. The Pharisee, standing by himself, prayed thus: 'God, I thank you that I am not like other men, extortioners, unjust, adulterers, or even like this tax collector. I fast twice a week; I give tithes of all that I get.' But the tax collector, standing far off, would not even lift up his eyes to heaven, but beat his breast, saying, 'God, be merciful to me, a sinner!' I tell you, this man went down to his house justified, rather than the other. For everyone who exalts himself will be humbled, but the one who humbles himself will be exalted."

Luke 18:10-14

Chapter 8

Objects May Appear Holier

My friend Pete (I changed his name) called me one day and told me he wanted to meet with me. I knew he was setting this appointment to share a concern he had with our church. I have been a pastor of this particular church for six years and it has been a difficult church. In fact, from the first month arriving I knew I was up against the current. Six years later I had survived up to three campaigns to push me out. Recently the poop hit the fan in our youth ministry and from this the efforts to remove me took on a new intensity but also a new face. To this point the malpots (You won't find that word on google. I made it up as my description of "them") were several men and women who wore no disguises. I could pick them out from a line up when I arrived. They were the ones who looked sternly when I preached, arms folded with brows that seemed to form the letters "you won't last long, buddy". They were the ones who would meet in little groups of threes after the service and immediately look away when I walked by. They were the ones who would meet with several elders to express their "concerns" that many others were unsettled. They were the ones who would collect letters and send them off in padded guaranteed overnight delivery mail to the district office.

Pete walked into my office with a friend. I grew tense when I greeted the friend since I had not been informed that he would be present. What made me even more tense, and I admit a bit defensive, were the two objects in Pete's two hands; an empty bucket and a milk jug of water. My friend gleefully informed me that he wanted to wash my feet. I shot back that while I loved the symbolism I felt awkward with all this. He assured me it would not hurt and would simply help all of us to come together in an attitude of humility. I chose to relax, took my shoes off and for the next few minutes allowed my friend to wash my feet... He leaned over toward me, smiled and said, "You need to resign from this Church. If you do God will take the devastating impact and turn it into amazing good. I have met with a hundred others in the church and they feel the same way." With the guidance and intervention of my superintendent I have resigned my position. **A male pastor with the Christian and Missionary Alliance.**

A few months after I received the above letter I received this follow up report from that same pastor.

I am the one that wrote you some months back about the footwashing incident that eventually led to our resigning our church. I thought it might be helpful to share with you what has happened since, confirming some of the things you wrote concerning the true intent of those who are adversarial in the church. About four months after this happened over 150 people left the church and the church is in serious financial water. I share this with you because again the "concern" from those who resisted us was that we were losing people and we were financially struggling. Interestingly several of those who were most aggressive have also left. I know you wrote that the real intent of these sort of sheep is really to destroy, and while I struggle that this could ever be true, our experience does confirm this. It's baffling and sad. I look forward to your next book.

A Carnival Mirror

Do you remember those mirrors in the funhouse at the carnival? Remember, they distort your reflection? I think they are a good metaphor describing the way the antagonists perceive their behavior. It is apparent that antagonists do not see themselves as they are. While it is difficult for victims of a sheep attack to understand, the following must be accepted as fact. The antagonists have honestly deceived themselves into believing that *"they are doing what is best for their church"*. In my consultations with parishes where antagonists were abusing successful clergy, I heard that statement repeated innumerable times. I heard it so often and so convincingly that I honestly believe that these personalities believe it themselves.

I will never forget meeting with two men and one woman that had targeted a rector for removal. That toxic parish had driven their last two rectors into early retirement. The three antagonists boasted that they'd had to *"straighten out the previous two rectors and now they had to straighten out the current one"*. They literally saw themselves as saviors of the parish. They were the good guys that needed to rid the congregation of the rectors who did not comply with their predetermined behavior pattern. They saw themselves as the smartest people in the congregation. They knew exactly what a good rector should look like, think and behave. Three successive clergy had failed to live up to their expectations. They believed themselves to be called by God Almighty, to use their words - *"to straighten those rectors out"*.

I received a telephone call from a rabbi who had given copies of *When Sheep Attack* to his board and some of the folks in the congregation that he believed were his supporters. The most hurtful response he received was from a man that he thought was one of his best friends. He said, *"I'm sorry you are taking all of this personally."*

"How can I not take it personally?" The rabbi asked. *"These people are trying to destroy me, my reputation, my very livelihood.*

They are attacking my character. They are giving no thought to how all this will affect my wife, my children or my ability to find employment in the future. It's very personal."

I remember consulting with one parish where a very wealthy man was unrelenting in his attacks on the senior minister. He pretended to be a man without sin. He even told me in a conversation over lunch at his exclusive club, *"I don't make mistakes and neither should the rector."* That night at dinner with some of the people supporting the pastor the conversation focused on that man. The senior warden summarized the consensus at the table, *"That crook should be in prison. He made his fortune by literally stealing from the widows and orphans in this town."*

I was told of a man in another parish that also pretended perfection and demanded the same of the rector. He even got elected to the vestry on the platform that he'd make sure everything was being done on *"the up and up".* Less than a year later the local newspaper and television channels carried the story of that man's arrest for burglary.

There was a woman in a parish that questioned the senior pastor's every word. She read ulterior motives into his sermons. She was just sure that he was *"up to no good".* In this case one of the associate clergy shed light on her behavior. *"She has never gotten over the fact that her husband left her for another woman. Once you get to know her you'll ask yourself what took him so long? She is so critical and controlling."*

These are but three examples of the antagonists living with their own dark secrets and projecting their darkness onto others. I would not want to conclude that all antagonists are portrayed in the behavior illustrated in these examples. The point I want to make is that a component of this behavior pattern is the inability to see their own imperfections.

The most forgiving hearts are the hearts that know their own need to be forgiven. The most judgmental are those that believe they are without sin. The judgmentalism, lack of compassion and forgiveness is exacerbated when the antagonist does in fact have dark secrets to hide. Their only recourse is to project those onto another. This is not a very large leap for those of us who subscribe to Carl Jung's understanding that we tend to project our dark shadows onto others so we don't have to deal with them in ourselves.

As a consultant for clergy under attack I consistently encountered antagonists that perceived themselves spiritually superior to their pastor and most of the congregation. This spiritual superiority carried a distinct pharisaical quality about it. Having found some perceived or real sin in their pastor they believed their actions were justified. There was no room for forgiveness, compassion or understanding. The pastor was forbidden to display even the smallest signs of human frailty. Over and over again I saw the words of Jesus validated regarding the splinter in the pastor's eye while ignoring the log in their own. The love that Jesus noted as the true mark of those that would follow him was completely absent. This was especially the case when it came to the pastors the antagonists targeted.

Healing Begins

Based on the findings presented in these case studies it appears that antagonists honestly see themselves and their actions as godly and virtuous. When they look in the mirror they see themselves as holier than their senior pastor and most everyone else.

Healing begins by not focusing on the pharisaic qualities exhibited by antagonists. Healing begins by returning to the basic disciplines of spirituality. Continue to develop the fruit of the spirit in your own life. The book of Galatians describes the fruit of the Spirit. They are listed as *love, joy, peace, patience, kindness, goodness, gentleness, faithfulness and self-control.* Healing begins by following the example of the publican in the story told by Jesus. Simply kneel and pray, *"God, be merciful to me, a sinner."*

For Reflection And Discussion

- Respond to the footwashing incident described in the opening letter.

- Is it possible the antagonists actually do see themselves as spiritually superior to the pastor and the other members of the congregation that support them? Again, agree or disagree and explain.

- Are clergy just being overly sensitive? Or are the attacks led by antagonists personal?

- Is there merit in the suggestion that the antagonists might be projecting their own dark shadows onto their pastor?

SECTION THREE

Understanding Why They Do It Helps A Little

"Finally, be strong in the Lord and in the strength of his might. Put on the whole armor of God, that you may be able to stand against the schemes of the devil. For we do not wrestle against flesh and blood, but against the rulers, against the authorities, against the cosmic powers over this present darkness, against the spiritual forces of evil in the heavenly places."
Ephesians 6:10-12

Chapter 9

Spiritual Warfare

I was in his car with him. We were driving down the freeway. He'd invited me to lunch. He looked over at me and said calmly, 'You know I am going to kill you!' I didn't know what to do. I couldn't jump out of the car. That would have been certain death. Then I got a break. He had to respond to the call of nature. He pulled into a rest stop. While he was in there I managed to get out of the car. There was a police substation near the rest stop. I ran in and told them what he'd said and where he was. They were waiting for him when he came out. Of course he denied threatening to kill me. It was my word against his but I knew I had to get away from him. I left that parish and moved to another city. I believed he was serious. He wanted me dead.
A male priest in The Episcopal Church

More than one pastor believed that they were engaged in a spiritual warfare with evil. The observation was stated in one form or another multiple times. *"I really did feel like I was up against the devil."* Others simply dismissed their antagonists as mean spirited. Still others saw their behavior as sinful motivated by jealousy.

I thought I was losing my mind. I honestly believed I was doing hand-to-hand combat with Satan. **A pastor in The Lutheran Church of America**

The spiritual component is ever so obvious. The words of Saint Paul resonate in these situations. In Galatians 5:19-26, he writes:

Now the works of the flesh are obvious: fornication, impurity, licentiousness, idolatry, sorcery, enmities, strife, ***jealousy, anger, quarrels, dissensions, factions, envy,*** *drunkenness, carousing, and things like these. I am warning you, as I warned you before: those who do such things will not inherit the kingdom of God. By contrast, the fruit of the Spirit is love, joy, peace, patience, kindness, generosity, faithfulness, gentleness, and self-control. There is no law against such things. And those who belong to Christ Jesus have crucified the flesh with its passions and desires. If we live by the Spirit, let us also be guided by the Spirit. Let us not become conceited, competing against one another, envying one another.*

Ultimately the question has to be asked – Is the antagonists' behavior evil? It's not a cruel question. It's not even meant to be a judgmental one. It is a question of spiritual discernment. It has been asked hundreds if not thousands of times by the victims of the antagonist's behavior and members of a multitude of congregations. As spiritual people who are required to distinguish between good and evil the question requires exploration even if no definitive answer is given. It is inherent in our Christian way of life to seek discernment by focusing on the behavior. The most commonly accepted definition of evil is *the willful intent to utterly destroy another person.* So is the antagonists' exhibited behavior evil? The question begs an answer.

I have resigned my cure. I will never return to the full time pastorate. I have met Satan in the form of three malicious men. I have confronted evil. Some say not. So let me put the question to you, Pastor Maynard. Is it evil to organize secret meetings designed to plot a pastor's downfall? Is it evil to use the Internet, vicious emails and letter writing campaigns filled with gossip and innuendo in an effort to destroy a man and his family? Is it evil to triangulate against a pastor with his bishop and other pastors for the sole purpose of devaluing them and their ministry? Is it evil to inflict anxiety, pain and suffering on the pastor's spouse and family? Is it evil to divide a congregation in order to get your way with no regard to the feelings or wishes of others? Is it evil to destroy a pastor's ministry and livelihood? I ask you kind sir.

If those things are not evil then just what is? **A pastor in The United Church of Canada.**

The sadistic quality inherent in the behavior of the antagonists has to be named and recognized. If allowed to have the taste of blood the first time their appetite becomes insatiable. They will continue to attack their old victims while looking for new ones. Compassion and charity may prevent us from naming their behavior as evil. It is at the very least sinful.

There was yet another aspect of the antagonist's behavior that appears confusing. It was repeatedly reported that often the antagonists were on the fringe of the parish life. Their attendance was sporadic at best. A review of their giving records reflected that their contributions were often minimal to non-existent. As the attacks on the senior pastor escalated they became more involved, often getting themselves elected to the board or vestry. Once it appeared that the pastor was going to leave they would resign their elected position. They then resumed their presence on the fringe of the parish. As one pastor described, *"It was as though they rode in from the country. Shot up the town. And once the damage was done they went back to the farm."* The question remains, why do they do what they do?

Healing Begins

Pastors are spiritual people. They are trained to believe that we humans are engaged in a spiritual warfare. There are forces of evil engaged in a brutal contest against the forces for good. Because pastors are also deeply compassionate people they are hesitant to label another person as evil. Christian Charity may prevent you from labeling the people that attacked you as evil. The behavior they exhibited carried all the marks. For many of the clergy in this study a critical part of their healing process included acknowledging that they had been engaged in a spiritual battle.

For Reflection and Discussion

- Is it unchristian to discern and name the behavior of the antagonists as evil? Why or why not?

- Do you believe in evil?

- Do you understand that pastors under attack may believe they are fighting with evil? How?

- How do people that are most often described as fringe members regarding their attendance and financial giving gain the necessary power to bring down a successful pastor?

"But when you enter a town and are not welcomed, go into its streets and say, 'Even the dust of your town we wipe from our feet as a warning to you. Yet be sure of this: The kingdom of God has come near.' I tell you it will be more bearable on that day for Sodom than for that town."
Luke 10:11

Chapter 10

Why Do They Do It?

One of the primary antagonists in the congregation described himself as a member of the most important two percent in the parish. He was a proud graduate of a university where he also served as a trustee. I once heard him describe the university as taking only the cream of the crop, but not the entire crop. He said the admissions committee would ever so slightly slide the tip of their finger across the top of the cream and those were the only ones they accepted. **A male priest in The Episcopal Church.**

Taylor Swift sings, *"Why you gotta be so mean?"* The question that haunts most people that have been targeted by antagonists is summarized in the title of this chapter. Why do they do it? Based on the cases that I've studied there are certain observations that can consistently be made.

The fact that is undeniable is that some two hundred plus clergy, church professionals, and lay leaders have painted a profile of their antagonists that includes specific behaviors. In our studies people in Protestantism, Roman Catholicism and the Jewish Faith describe these behaviors. The behaviors are consistent whether coming from conservative or liberal congregations. The descriptions from men and women are the same. As was stated in *When Sheep Attack* the behavior profile includes:

- High control needs
- A sense of entitlement
- Anger that can explode into rage
- Jealousy of the senior minister's success and popularity
- Easily hurt feelings
- Insensitivity to the feelings of other people
- Inability to admit their own mistakes

Also mentioned was suspicion of alcohol abuse or the recognition that their antagonists were either recovering or active alcoholics. One Baptist preacher described the behavior with the classic, *"For them, it was their way or the highway."*

Narcissistic Personality Disorder

The question, *"Why are they doing this?"* was asked of me too many times to ignore. I had the opportunity to ask Rabbi Edwin Friedman (*Generation To Generation* - Guilford Publishing) that very question not long before his death. His reply was classic, *"Some people are just mean S.O.B.s!"* (The acronym is mine).

If that answer was enough for the good Rabbi it should have been good enough for me, but pastoral curiosity wanted more. I wanted a clinical answer. For that I turned to the experts in the fields of mental health and addiction. I presented them with the behavior pattern of the antagonists as developed in the case studies I had reviewed. They gave me the following as possible explanations.

Those that work with alcohol and addiction recovery found a correlation with what they term *dry drunk behavior.* I was pointed to Narcissistic Personality Disorder by the psychologists I consulted. The behavior patterns for each are more than coincidental with those of the antagonists. It really doesn't take a doctorate in psychology or psychiatry to see the similarities between the behavior patterns of the antagonists and persons living with Narcissistic Personality Disorder. The patterns are just too close to one another to dismiss as pop psychology.

The Diagnostic and Statistical Manual of Mental Disorders used by mental health professionals list the following behaviors for people living with Narcissistic Personality Disorder.

*Self-centered
*Seek constant attention and admiration
*Consider themselves better than others

* Believe they are entitled to special treatment
* Unreasonable control needs
* Are easily hurt but may not see that in themselves
* Unable to hear another's viewpoint
* Insensitive to the feelings of others
* Envy and jealousy
* Take advantage of others to achieve their own goals
* May suffer with alcohol or substance abuse

It needs to be noted that at this writing the DSM is undergoing some revisions for the publication of DSM 5. Narcissistic Personality Disorder is only one part of a continuum that encompasses other personality impairments. That is the prevailing view by those doing the work. The behavioral disorder is also a matter of degree. Some folks may display only minimal behavioral traits while others have developed them to the extreme. The defining criteria are subject to both expansion and inclusion with other disorders. Currently, the proposals for diagnosing NPD interpersonal functioning include the following language.

Empathy: impaired ability to recognize or identify with the feelings and needs of others.

Intimacy: relationships largely superficial and exist to serve self-esteem.

Antagonism: characterized by:
    entitlement,
    self-centeredness,
    condescending toward others.

Attention seeking: excessive attempts to attract and be the focus of attention.

Requires excessive admiration: If that is not received they want to be feared and perceived as notorious.

Demand automatic and full compliance to their demands.

They "use" others to achieve their ends.

Driven with envy of others and seeks to hurt or destroy those they envy.

When challenged they will display violent rage.

NPD is seldom a solitary diagnosis and most often is accompanied by yet other disorders in this category.

The characteristics of NPD exacerbate with age and the restrictions the passing years place on the individual.

As the conversations around the DSM 5 evolve, the similarities between the behavior patterns of the antagonists and those living with NPD become even more apparent. Antagonists clearly perceive themselves to be the smartest people in the room. One antagonist that considered himself an expert on leadership best summed it up in this statement he made to the governing board. *"I told the pastor what he needed to do. I told him he needed to write more thank you notes. He needed to smile more. And his wife should stop sitting in the back of the church. She should sit up front. In fact, there is usually an open pew right in front of me. He hasn't done a single one of them. He doesn't know the first thing about leadership. I tried to help him but he simply won't listen. I don't care for him. I no longer have any use for him. He needs to go."*

We all possess healthy narcissism. It's important to recognize that these are not the characteristics of a healthy narcissism driven by an internal sense of self-improvement and accomplishment. The behavior pattern the DSM is designed to diagnose is a pathological narcissism. It is a lifelong behavior pattern mirroring an obsession with oneself to the exclusion of all others. One can attribute the expression, *"to hell with everyone else, I want what I want and I want it right now"* to the pathological narcissists. It is a textbook example of the ruthless pursuit of one's self gratification and heaven help anyone that gets in their way. There are degrees of narcissism and various mental health professionals divide them into varying categories. There is one category in particular that I believe is applicable to understanding antagonists.

Closet Narcissist

The category of narcissism that I was directed to study by the psychologists is known as *Closet Narcissism.* It appears to best match the profile for those that act out in the Church. James Masterson, M. D. in his book *The Search For The Real Self* (The Free Press – New York) describes this category. The *Closet Narcissist* seeks out a group or institution that they can use to feed their narcissism. Often for these folks it is the Church. It is important to understand that for this type of narcissist there is no "other". There are no boundaries. Their church is but an extension of their own ego. When they say *"my church"* they literally mean *"my church".* It is their church to the exclusion of others. While they donate money to their church it still remains **their money.** That means they are entitled to control how it is utilized. But it goes further. They also believe that other's donations should also be under their control. Their money remains their money and your money belongs to them as well.

In *When Sheep Attack* I described a bishop that became infamous for his poison pen letters. Even after leaving The Episcopal Church and founding his own schismatic denomination he continued to attack those that he had identified as his enemies. He was especially brutal in his letters and remarks about bishops and clergy that had publicly challenged his opposition to the ordination of women. That bishop's behavior is a textbook example of a *Closet Narcissist*. Narcissists at all levels either see other people in their lives as a mirroring object that reflects good on them, an attacking object or they so devalue them as being inferior to them that they do not exist at all.

From that frame of reference it's easy to see that if the Church or one of Her leaders does not mirror favorably on them then they either devalue it or attack them. In the bishop's scenario, The Episcopal Church had started ordaining women contrary to his image of what it should do. Because his opposition had been so public, the Episcopal Church and her leaders ceased to mirror favorably on him.

He continued to try to control the governance of the church even though he had been removed from the denomination. He attempted to do so by attacking and devaluing the ministries of the bishops and priests that had dared to publicly disagree with him. They and The Episcopal Church failed to feed his narcissism so he went on the attack. That is the classic example of an antagonist at work, i.e. *Closet Narcissists*. The *Closet Narcissist* sees the senior pastor as an extension of themselves. The senior pastors are not entitled to their own preferences. They are, by design, an integral part of **their congregation** and therefore are but an extension of the ego of the narcissist. When a person fails to mirror favorably on them they attack. More often than not they will feed their pawns false information and get them to do their dirty work for them. Most *Closet Narcissists* prefer to work under the radar and sign their work – *anonymous*. The following letter was slipped under the door of my hotel room. The night before I had led my first session with the vestry of a conflicted parish.

My dear Dennis, I trust you will allow me to call you by your baptismal name. I have an aversion to the titles you clergy choose to use. I find "reverend" to be quite pretentious. I find "father" to be a direct contradiction to our Lord's teachings. I refuse to call any man "father". Now that is settled I need to enlighten you.

I choose to give you the benefit of the doubt. I believe from the reports I've received from last night's meeting your intentions are pure albeit, quite misdirected. I've known N a lot longer than you. He has attempted to be rector of our parish over the past three years but has failed miserably. There are certain facts not in evidence that only a few of us possess. The long and short of it is that N does not possess the leadership qualities or skills our parish needs. You can best serve this congregation by encouraging him to resign post haste.

Several of us have already canceled our pledges. I can assure you that many more are to follow if he does not resign. Once he has submitted his resignation we will be more than happy to significantly increase our giving to the parish. I perceive you to be a bright man despite the deficiencies and limitations of the educational institutions you attended.

Yes, I have read your book. I choose to dismiss it as the ramblings of twenty-five clergy that should have been fired long before their ministries ended. Had you spent more time interviewing their congregational leaders you would have known that.

Now that you have been enlightened I trust you will treat the parish equitably and earn the considerable consulting fee you are charging us. I think that you need only to encourage N to accept the six weeks severance he has been offered and you will have done your job.

The letter was unsigned.

Healing Begins

This possible diagnosis or explanation for the behavior of the antagonists can help - a little. It doesn't change the reality of the situation. It doesn't take away any of the pain. It does allow the mind to possibly begin to make sense of it all. So far as that is helpful it can contribute to the healing. But healing is a matter for the heart.

What if Narcissistic Personality Disorder is a credible explanation for the behavior of the antagonists? Would that open new avenues for bishops, denominational authorities and parish leaders to manage their behavior? Granted it would require even more education and training than this cursory look. The mental health professionals only presented it to me as a possible explanation. But for just this healing moment, imagine the possibilities.

For Reflection and Discussion

- Is comparing the behavior pattern of the antagonists with Narcissistic Personality Disorder just pop psychology or does it have some merit? Why or why not?

- Doctor Masterson states that *Closet Narcissists* seek out a group or institution to feed their needs. What factors make the Church an attractive choice for them?

- Why would people living with Narcissistic Personality Disorder be antagonistic to a pastor that is successfully turning around a declining congregation?

- Respond to the statement that the Narcissistic Antagonists views their pastor as an extension of themselves.

"For I am sure that neither death nor life, nor angels nor rulers, nor things present nor things to come, nor powers, nor height nor depth, nor anything else in all creation, will be able to separate us from the love of God in Christ Jesus our Lord."
Romans 8:38 - 39

Chapter 11

Antagonists Are In Pain

Mental health professionals recognize that narcissistic personalities are among the most difficult to treat. Likewise, a relationship with them is troublesome. The narcissists are consumed with their own image and point of view. Couple that with the unshakeable belief that they can do no wrong and you have the foundation for an unmovable object. Most all authorities agree that having a relationship with a narcissist is not practical.

Those with NPD appear to be incapable of understanding the devastation their acting out brings to their parish and their pastor. The most obvious evidence for this is that when allowed their behavior will be repeated. The evidence that their hurtful behavior meets an obsessive need deep inside their psyche can be heard in their boasting. *"We got rid of her." "We got the goods on that so-called preacher." "We fired him."* Further evidence that they are driven can be seen in their obsession with their target years, even decades, after they have won the local battle. That is one of the elements in the profile of the antagonist that caught my attention. They never seem to be satisfied with their victory.

Even after they have bullied a pastor into leaving a parish they will continue to haunt them. They will continue to pursue them. Years, even decades later, they will continue to try to destroy the pastor in the eyes of others. They will even follow them into retirement and beyond. Through it all they appear to be completely oblivious to the destructive nature of their behavior. They have no empathy for the pastor or the pastor's family. They are unsympathetic to the other members of the parish that leave the Church because of their behavior. In their world there are certain members that are important and there are those that are quite literally disposable. They wave their hand dismissively, *"They don't matter. Let them go."* So exactly what drives this behavior?

It is for these reasons that I have come to the conclusion that antagonists are driven. They are responding to an inner compulsion. The people that target a pastor for removal are hurting. Just consider how tiring it must be for them to always have to be right. They must win every argument. It must be exhausting to have to compete with every person they envy. Add to all that, the need to continually be in control of every situation and every person encountered twenty-four hours a day - seven days a week.

Every clergy person who has ever been targeted by antagonists can see their pain. They've seen the panic on their faces when they fear they are not the center of attention. The volcanic anger in their voices when confronted is undeniable. They cannot hide from the pastor their desperate need to be in control. The looks of envy at the pastor's success and popularity are undeniable. The antagonists are victims of their own internal pain. They are obsessed with the need to fill the hole that is in their hearts. That hole demands that they be in control, center stage and recipients of all praise and popularity being lavished. God help anyone that they believe is upstaging them.

People frequently want to anesthetize their pain. Alcoholism is often an ingredient in the antagonist's profile. The alcohol doesn't take away the pain. It only exacerbates the abusive behavior. When the pain of the antagonists becomes too much for them they act out by striking out. The behavioral profile of the antagonist is very similar to the profile of those living with any personality disorder. The people with personality disorders are living in pain. Their behavior is driven by the desire to satisfy a need and find a way to stop hurting. Often they are unaware of what they are doing. Mistakenly they believe that their pain will end by hurting another.

They Don't Just Act Out In The Church

While clergy antagonists are the focus of this book and my previous ones it needs to be observed that this behavior is not restricted to the Church. Persons living with NPD don't just act out in religious communities. Over and over again I heard stories of these same people's behavior at the country club, civic club, Home Owner's Association and yes, in their workplaces. Many had already earned a reputation for targeting managers of clubs, heads of schools, museum directors and symphony conductors. Antagonists are not just antagonists at Church. My studies indicate that their behavior also leads to dysfunctional relationships in their families, including those with their spouses and children. Their need for ego gratification can be so insatiable that they are unable to even enjoy or celebrate the accomplishments of their own spouse or children. They must turn those around so that they reflect favorably on them. The antagonist has to be center stage. I received the following email from a physician that more than illustrates this point.

I had the pleasure of reading your book "When Sheep Attack!" I grew up Lutheran, but recently had been attending an Episcopal church. As I read the book, I felt like I was looking into a mirror. The description of bullying in the book is so true and yet often put under the rug. It is the elephant in the room no one wants to talk about. But this "elephant" is destructive.
The book was a mirror, not so much for

experiences in church life, but rather it reflected my experiences as a medical student.

In spite of the esteem physicians are given, the medical world is fraught with similar bullying. A successful doctor or resident might also be overworked and exhausted. Others are filled with envy, and become "antagonists." That hapless doctor might be held to a "perfectionist" standard in an attempt to cast a shadow on his record. Eventually he might be ousted with a tarnished reputation filled with accusations and rumors. Even if false, they have done their damage. The same goes for residents and occasionally medical students.

I know one who was bullied out of his job due to outright jealousy. He had a successful practice. He was clearly intelligent, affable, and hardworking. He was religious, and we connected because of this. His coworkers were instructed to find "dirt" on him. After they tarnished his reputation, he was terminated and was replaced ironically by the doctor who investigated him

Similar to clergy, doctors are not confrontational, seeking to reconcile and find common ground. Doctors carry the image of caring and compassion. Not at all like the rambunctiousness of a marine.

I particularly enjoyed the book's practical approach. Just as a Bishop plays a role, the "higher ups" above a doctor/resident can save his career. Just as some churches have a history of this, some hospitals too have a history of this. Sometimes the only solution is to find a new parish... many times doctors leave a hospital because that is the only recourse.

Doctors/residents often become cynical, paranoid, and angry. They burn out and many times flee the practice. Unknown to most people are the divorce, the alcoholism, drug abuse, and damaged lives many health professionals have. This is especially true among surgeons. Shows on television like "House" glamorize this, but this is an awful reality.

While I feel saddened that these things happen among clergy... especially a church I feel so at home in, I found some solace in hearing similar stories. Also, I can't help but feel some similarity between these stories and Joseph in Genesis. **A male Doctor of Medicine.**

The Critical One Percent

In the clinical environment between two and sixteen percent of the patients undergoing treatment will be diagnosed with NPD. In the general population approximately one percent of a given community will be people living with NPD. At first, one percent doesn't sound all that threatening. But consider the now two hundred plus cases that compose this study. Consistently the number of people that abused the senior pastor or religious professional into leaving was just a handful. Often it was stated there were only two or three of them, but they were brutal and unrelenting. One percent of the typical pastoral parish would be just a couple of people. One percent of a program size parish would be five or six. Therein lies the frustration. A pastor and a congregation of one hundred and fifty members destroyed by two or three people living with a personality disorder! Or consider that eight or ten people that make up the one percent can bring down a parish of a thousand. The one percent statistic found in every congregation in the Church Catholic or any gathered community is a fact that we ignore to our own peril.

An old Peanuts comic strip included this scene. Lucy is swinging on the playground. Charlie Brown reads to her, *"It says here that the world revolves around the sun once a year."* Lucy stops abruptly and responds, *"The world revolves around the sun? Are you sure? I thought it revolved around me."*

It is up to the reader to determine whether or not the behavior of their particular antagonists corresponds to the behavior of persons living with Narcissistic Personality Disorder. I cannot do that for you. I can only call your attention to this possibility. It is difficult to deny the similarities between the behavior profiles for antagonists and persons living with Narcissistic Personality Disorder. As with all personality disorders the severity of the disorder is a matter of degree. Some behavioral characteristics may tend to be more exaggerated than others. Some may be more severe in one person than they are in another. After all is said and done, whether the behavior pattern of the antagonists in your situation corresponds to that of persons living with NPD can only allow us to understand them better. Clearly, we would not consider the behavior that seeks to destroy another person using any method available as normal. I am offering Narcissistic Personality Disorder as a possible explanation for just why antagonists do what they do.

    I honestly believe the antagonists in my research suffer with a behavioral disorder that prevents them from coming to terms with the destructive nature of their behavior. I choose to give them that grace. That does not mean, however, that I believe the Church or any parish in the Church should tolerate their behavior. While they cannot be fixed, leaders must confront and manage their behavior. If the leaders of the Church and the parishes within it continue to allow them to hold the Church hostage, the future is irreversible. More and more clergy and their families will be severely damaged. Growing congregations will experience decline. And multiple laypersons that were once faithful and enthusiastic about the Church and their parish will simply walk away. It appears they will never return.

    How much damage can a handful of people do? The Church is littered with sparsely attended congregations. I have been able to document multiple clergy that have been so beaten up their physical, emotional and spiritual health has been destroyed. And then there is the multitude of once faithful lay people so damaged by the antagonist's handiwork they will never return to any church. The evidence is all around us.

The spiritual leaders of all worshipping communities must open their eyes and act accordingly. Persons that are suffering with a personality disorder must not be allowed to hold communities of faith and their pastors hostage. This is even more critical when we understand that they appear to be incapable of comprehending the destructive ramifications of their own actions. They even appear to be incapable of seeking help for themselves. Mental health professionals would say they are *out of control*. It is ironic. **In their effort to control others they appear to be unable to control their own behavior.** If this is in fact the case then Church leaders must learn how to manage their behavior for them.

Healing Begins

Pastors are by nature compassionate individuals. Through education and training their empathetic skills are sharpened even further. Clergy empathize with people in pain every day of their lives. Their hearts go out to those engaging in self-destructive behavior.

With every fiber of their being a pastor wants to help those who are hurting. Antagonists are hurting. They are not happy people. Their behavior is not restricted to the worshipping community. Their controlling and abusive behavior is also unleashed on their spouse, their children and any person that challenges them. These studies indicate that a great many of them are also suffering with addiction to alcohol.

Healing begins by returning to the very basic tenets of pastoral education. *There are certain people that you can help. There are others that can be helped, but not by you. Then there are those that cannot be helped at all because they don't want to be helped.* You could not help the antagonists that attacked you.

For Reflection and Discussion

- Do you believe antagonists are victims of their own pain? Why or why not?

- Do you think the antagonists become jealous of their pastor's popularity and success? Why or why not?

- If Narcissistic Personality Disorder cannot explain the behavior of antagonists, then what other explanation would you offer?

- Have you even seen the work of a group of antagonists in an organization outside the Church? Describe what happened.

SECTION FOUR

Healing Brings New Life

"I will restore you to health and heal your wounds," declares the Lord, "because you are called an outcast."
Jeremiah 30:17

Chapter 12

The Severely Wounded

I wanted to let you know just how encouraged I have been since I read your book, 'When Sheep Attack'. My husband has been a senior pastor for the past thirty-three years. About five years ago, when our church was flourishing and had just built a large new facility and was totally debt free... we were forced to resign.

We could have been one of your twenty-five churches in the study you did. Everything resonated with us. I was reading portions to my husband, and we just couldn't get over the similarities.

Thank your for taking the time and love to care for wounded clergy and to write such an eye-opening account. Somehow knowing that we were not alone... knowing that we were not the only ones 'blind-sighted', was so very helpful. We always keep saying to one another... 'What happened??!' We just didn't understand.

We are ok. God has been good to us and has sustained us. We, however, did not have any idea the toll that this would take on others and us. Five years later, we still are sort of in shock, but trust the Lord to have used this to make us more like His precious Son, Jesus.

May the Lord bless your efforts, as you have sought to care for others! **A minister's wife in The Church of Christ.**

From time to time I choose to make the ninety-minute drive over to Los Angeles. One of my sons lives there, but I also enjoy the many opportunities that city offers. When I leave the Coachella Valley the sky is blue and clear, but as I approach Los Angeles I often see a large yellow cloud enveloping the skyline. That cloud is the infamous Los Angeles smog. What I find interesting is that once I enter that cloud I forget about it. The sky appears to be blue and the air cooled by the ocean breeze smells fresh. It's not until I am on my way back home and I look back at the city in my rearview mirror do I see that yellow cloud again.

I've often thought of that cloud as a perfect metaphor for living inside a toxic parish. The critical and negative atmosphere becomes so familiar that it begins to feel normal. Aren't all parishes like this? Don't all clergy walk on eggshells as they go about their daily ministries? Doesn't every clergy person have a few members constantly critiquing their every move? Aren't there negative people continually nipping at all pastors' heels like little dogs? The anxious feeling in the chest and pit of the stomach becomes a cruel companion. The disapproving looks and the constant criticism are just part of the job. The daily tension-filled meetings are dreaded but necessary.

Often it is not until a pastor leaves that atmosphere they realize the toxic environment that has surrounded them. It is only when they have entered a healthy atmosphere and look back they realize just how really sick it was. Rare is the individual, lay or ordained, that comes through this experience without being wounded. The lucky ministers are old enough to retire. Some are fortunate to find a new and healthy congregation. The positive atmosphere will give them the love and healing they need to continue to exercise a fruitful ministry. Many become professional interim clergy. Again, depending on the parish, this ministry can bring them healing. The most unfortunate are those that are forced to enter the world of unemployment. Thanks to the rumor mill the antagonists so enjoy feeding, these unfortunate pastors too often become unemployable in the Church.

The German language has a word that I think best describes the atmosphere in today's world and consequently the Church. It is *zeitgeist*. It translates *the spirit of the times*. The spirit of our times is especially brutal for any who aspire to leadership. The pettiness of the political arena is now mirrored in the Church. This is all driven by the craze for investigative journalism, supermarket tabloids and the loss of factual news reporting. The current zeitgeist provides all the camouflage the antagonists need to do their work. With the enthusiasm of cub reporters antagonists delight in dumpster diving into a clergy person's past. Flying beneath the flag of holiness and piety decades of personal history will be examined with a fine toothed comb. Nothing is off limits. Even the personal history of a clergy person's spouse can become fair game.

That is the very reason that I believe that all pastors should have an alternative career plan – Plan B. After doing battle with the antagonists, clergy may not find continuing in any form of ministry desirable. Unemployed clergy will discover that two or three advanced degrees in theology are not very marketable in the larger economy. If you hold licenses, degrees, or credentials that supported your family before entering the ministry, it would be wise to keep them current.

Regardless of the ministry or career path chosen following a battle with the antagonists, my studies indicate that the pastor and often their spouse will suffer physically, emotionally and spiritually. The two most traumatic results of a sheep attack for them are either burnout or post traumatic stress disorder. When the trauma has been particularly severe it can produce a combination of both. The following may also apply to lay professionals, church musicians, and members of the congregation that have been on the frontlines against a sheep attack.

Chronic Stress

I am not a clinical psychologist. Nor do I have any degrees or training in medicine. As a pastor to wounded clergy I've had to expand my knowledge in both arenas. I have been fortunate to have licensed professionals in both fields guide me. The following observations are made with that caveat. If nothing else the following will encourage you to increase your own knowledge in these areas. In particular I would encourage you to learn more about the following topics: Chronic Stress and the role that the hormone Cortisol plays in our health, Emotional Memory Storage, Burnout and Post Traumatic Stress Injury. Any one of them could justify an entire book. I want only to raise your awareness of the role they play in the lives of the victims of sheep attacks.

Canadian physician David Posen sounds the alarm for every person under constant stress in his book, *Is Work Killing You? A Doctor's Prescription for Treating Workplace Stress* (Anansi Press). He points to the dangers surrounding the hormone Cortisol. The body secretes this hormone when placed under stress. It is particularly needed when we enter a "fight or flight" situation. It heightens our senses and gives us the shot that we need to respond as needed. It works to our advantage when the situation is brief and short lived. Mental health professionals term such situational moments as "acute stress".

However, when our body is exposed too frequently and with too much intensity to "fight or flight" over an extended period of time it cannot reset itself. It remains in a state of heightened awareness waiting for the enemy to attack. This is known as "chronic stress". Our body remains in the "fight or flight" mode. A prolonged increase in the hormone Cortisol has a negative impact on a person's overall health. In particular it has been observed to do the following among others:

> Impair cognitive performance
> Raise Blood Pressure
> Lower immunity
> Raise the levels of LDL - bad cholesterol
> Lower levels of HDL - good cholesterol
> Increase stomach fat

It has been shown that the increase in LDL and the lowering of HDL along with the increase in stomach fat are major contributors to heart attacks and stroke. It has also been shown that a lowered immune system makes the body more vulnerable to all types of disease, including cancer.

Pastors, lay professionals and lay leaders subjected to chronic stress at the hands of the antagonists become prime candidates for this increase in Cortisol. Read again some of the letters from those that have been subjected to the bullying, intimidation and threats of the antagonists. Their abuse often extended for weeks, months and in some cases years. This only brings forth the following question. How many victims of a sheep attack have developed high blood pressure, had a stroke, a heart attack, been diagnosed with cancer or some other physical infirmity in the first few months or year following the attack? As for the impaired cognitive function, those pastors under attack consistently reported that they were feeling mentally paralyzed, helpless, and unable to process the rumors and charges being levied against them.

Emotional Memories

Researchers at the University of Zurich have demonstrated that emotional memories, both positive and negative, are stored in our brains in a particular way. They point out that there is a big difference between emotional memories and learned knowledge. Facts or learned knowledge can completely vanish from memory. At one time I could recite the capitols of all fifty states within a few minutes. When challenged to do so today it will take me longer and I am certain to have forgotten a few.

Emotional memories are not so easily forgotten. Extreme emotional recollections remain stored for a whole lifetime. The researchers point out that the brain imprints traumatic experiences as "feeling states". The feelings of fear, helplessness, horror and anxiety are stored as "living emotions". These "feeling states" are then timeless. As such the adverse memories can hinder the way we go about our lives. We tend to avoid those places, smells, objects or people that remind us of the trauma. Encountering any one of them can bring those feelings of helplessness, fear, horror and anxiety forward with all the intensity that they were experienced during the event itself. It is not surprising that a smell, song, place or person triggered the flashbacks and nightmares reported in this study. It is equally obvious to note the need for victims of a sheep attack to avoid any thing, place or person that would awaken those traumatic feelings.

Burnout

I was a pastor for over thirty years. I thought my last congregation was a gem. It was an enviable assignment. In less than a year after my arrival the criticism began. I dreaded board meetings because I knew a couple of the members would bring complaints about me they'd heard from anonymous sources. A couple of antagonists, not elected to the board, attended every meeting. I knew they were there in an effort to intimidate me.

I'd heard rumors of secret meetings being led by the now retired former pastor. Your book told the rest of my story. Anonymous letters, phone calls and death threats accompanied canceled pledges.

The greater congregation appeared to be unaware of any of this. Our average Sunday attendance, giving and membership actually continued to increase. Four years into my ministry in that congregation a slate of four were elected to the board. Things went from bad to worse so I took early retirement.

It's been almost three years since I retired. I've not gone to worship one time. I hadn't missed a Sunday since I was a college student. I just can't bring myself to go. I feel so empty inside. I have no desire to be a part of any Church in any capacity. I start to pray but my words fail me. My wife tries to get me to do things in our retirement, but I just don't feel up to it. My doctor has me on an anti-depressant. I guess it's helping but I can't really tell.

I gave my life to the Church only to have it betray me. I just wish that someone would tell me what I did that was so wrong. **A retired male pastor in The United Methodist Church.**

Burnout is the product of being subjected to unrelenting stress and anxiety over a period of time. When a person feels overworked, undervalued and unappreciated they become a candidate for burnout. Other contributing factors to burnout include a lack of recognition for achievements, conflicting expectations, and losing control over one's work responsibilities. The person begins to feel disillusioned, helpless and exhausted. Their emotions will include feelings of being trapped and defeated. A sense of failure dominates their waking and often sleeping thoughts. My dear reader, is that not a precise description of the experience ministers being attacked by antagonists live through?

A person will begin to realize that they are suffering with burnout when they cease to even have the energy to care. Their cynicism and hopelessness is compounded by feelings of resentment. Burnout also fills a person with self-doubt. The metaphor for burnout is a burned out house with a person sitting inside looking out. The exterior of the house is intact and may appear unharmed. The interior, however, is destroyed. It is empty. There is nothing usable left.

A burned out person is chronically tired and will suffer with a low grade to persistent depression. They will have difficulty sleeping and will have either lost an interest in food or turn to food to negate the pain they feel. Headaches and gastrointestinal disturbances plague them. The passion and energy they formerly had for their profession or institution is gone.

One cannot recover from burnout by taking a few days off work. A brief or even an extended vacation alone will not bring a person out of their burned out state. Recovering from burnout will take time. The first step is to give yourself permission to rest, reflect, and heal. The temptation is to isolate oneself during burnout. If a person is going to recover from the damage done to them physically, psychologically and spiritually they need their family and friends. Sharing your hurt and feelings with the people that love you is an essential part of the healing process.

The most difficult part of the recovery process involves acknowledging your losses. There is a certain amount of idealism that leads men and women to ordination. That same idealism is shared with lay professionals and laity that become active in faith communities. A sheep attack pours water all over that sacred fire. There is also the loss of friends in your former congregation. If the gossip and slander around your leaving has been particularly ferocious there is the loss of esteem, respect and professionalism. It's like a death. There is the death of idealism. The ministry that was so fulfilling feels empty. At the heart of the Gospel is the resurrection of Jesus. He has conquered death.

Post Traumatic Stress Disorder (Injury)

Thank you for your book "When Sheep Attack". I got a death threat, someone ransacked my office, and another person planted child pornography on my office computer. And, of course, there were the attacks on my character, on that of my wife and children. And this was all done in the name of orthodoxy. I had a very supportive Bishop, but since these people hated him as much as me there was not much to do. The vestry was completely unprepared and when I coached them on how to stand up to the group they ignored my advice and essentially hung me out to dry. I left soon afterwards. Then the wrath was turned on the vestry and they finally got backbone, but too late for me. And you are right. This all took place in a rapidly growing successful parish where everything was on the upswing. I stole no money, slept with no parishioners, yet I was run out of town as if I had caused the greatest scandal in history. Some people publicly accused me of being in league with Satan. I was completely surprised by the level of Post Traumatic Stress Disorder I encountered. It took eighteen months to get over the panic attacks I felt just before saying the opening service each Sunday at the early service. **A male priest in The Episcopal Church**

PTSD is most often associated with wartime soldiers or victims of a violent crime. People that have witnessed a particularly horrific event are often diagnosed with PTSD. This disorder is the product of an event that so traumatized them as to produce emotional paralysis. PTSD is developed when a person's safety is threatened.

Consider the number of ministers in this study that received death threats either directly or anonymously. PTSD is developed when the individual is rendered helpless. Consider again the number that reported they just didn't know what their antagonists were going to do next. PTSD is the result of being subjected to an event that was unpredictable and uncontrollable. Consider the stories of those that reported the attacks were a surprise or unexpected.

PTSD leaves the individual feeling anxious, frightened, and disconnected. They are stuck with the painful memories. They are experiencing psychological shock. Repeatedly reliving the traumatic event through flashbacks and nightmares is one of the most common symptoms of PTSD. The person can literally be going about their daily routine years after the event and a flashback of some aspect of the painful event will wash over them like a tsunami. PTSD victims will have reoccurring nightmares of the event years even decades after the event itself. These flashbacks and nightmares produce intense physical reactions, which include a pounding heart, a rise in blood pressure, rapid breathing, and nausea. They can be plagued with unexpected and seemingly uncontrollable bouts of anger. Those that live with PTSD have a difficult time moving forward with their lives. Extreme mood swings often plague them. They tend to avoid activities, places, thoughts or feelings that remind them of the trauma.

Consider all the stories of the clergy and laity that have been a part of this study. Consider the number of pastors that no longer want anything to do with the Church in any form. Consider the number that avoid any thing, place or person that brings back memories of the pain.

I am pleased to note that those charged with writing the *Fifth Edition of the Diagnostic and Statistical Manual Of Mental Disorders* are proposing that Post Traumatic Stress Disorder be changed to Post Traumatic Stress Injury. Those that have been subjected to long periods of abuse and trauma have been injured! Pastors that have been abused by people within their own congregations are injured. They share all the same symptoms as any person subjected to emotional trauma. So it is not surprising that many of the clergy and religious professionals that have been a part of my studies sought treatment for post traumatic stress disorder – PTSD.

Self-treatment is not recommended. The symptoms of PTSD often appear within hours or days of the events. In some cases they may not appear until months or years after the trauma. Early treatment is best! Symptoms of PTSD may grow worse if not treated. There are some studies that show there is a strong relationship between PTSD and symptomatic high blood pressure and cardiac trouble. Treatment should be sought as soon as the symptoms appear. A qualified therapist and spiritual director will be required in order to recover. Medication to help relieve anxiety and depression may also be required. These may help minimize the symptoms but therapy is required to treat the causes.

There is one dangerous temptation for those experiencing burnout or PTSD. It is to believe that finding a new congregation to serve will bring healing. It is imperative that your invisible wounds be treated with the same care as any open wound. You will need time to heal. That includes time away from the stress of daily ministry. As every pastor knows, the emotional volleyball of ministering to even the most loving congregation can be exhausting. Leaving one energy-draining situation in order to enter what potentially could be another will not bring the needed healing. It will only exacerbate your burnout or PTSD further. Your body, your mind and yes, your spirit need time to heal.

Healing Begins

The concept of the Sabbath finds its origin in early scripture. Resting on the seventh day so that the mind and body could re-create themselves. Allowing the land to rest every seven years so that it could heal and then become productive once again. For those that have been severely wounded by a sheep attack some form of the Sabbath may just be what is needed. The following may sound counter intuitive and perhaps even a bit sacrilegious. But the clergy and lay leaders that I interviewed found that taking time away from the Church - all churches - was one of the best things they did for their own healing.

For Reflection and Discussion

- Do you think it's possible to be in a toxic parish and think that it is normal? Why or why not?

- Does the description of burnout sound like you or someone you know? Can lay members that have been through a sheep attack also burn out?

- Do you believe that the turmoil of a sheep attack could be so traumatic as to bring Post Traumatic Stress Injury to a pastor? Why or why not?

- Could burnout or PTSD explain those that no longer want anything to do with the Church? Why or why not?

"And I heard a loud voice from the throne saying, "Look! God's dwelling place is now among the people, and he will dwell with them. They will be his people, and God himself will be with them and be their God. 'He will wipe every tear from their eyes. There will be no more death or mourning or crying or pain, for the old order of things has passed away."
Revelation 21:3-4

Chapter 13

Healing Begins

One of the questions that I asked of those that I interviewed surrounded the methods they were using to heal. A distinct pattern appeared. It seems that recovering from a sheep attack involves returning to the basics of the spiritual life. The tools that will strengthen you to move forward and bring healing are the same ones that the faithful have used through the centuries. In order to regain wholeness the wounded reported that they focused on these ancient disciplines. Sadly, it was consistently reported that the individual bishops and denominational officers provided no support or pastoral care for the victims of the sheep attacks. Some reported they even felt like they had become "outcasts" or "untouchables" in the eyes of their church officials.

I received a call to another parish in a distant state. After the movers left we loaded up the minivan and followed them down the highway. One of the most beautiful sights I've ever seen in my life was the skyline of that city in my rearview mirror. **A male pastor in The United Church of Christ.**

The following is not intended to be an exhaustive list of healing tools. These five were the ones most frequently mentioned by the clergy and lay leaders I interviewed.

1. Accept and implement Jesus' instructions to shake the dust off your feet. Well, not literally. The first step in the healing process that was consistently reported was to separate from the antagonists and the parish that surrounds them. All reported it was tempting to want to know what people were saying. How badly has the attendance declined? Are they losing pledges? Who else has left the parish? None of that proved helpful to their healing. Staying involved in the life of their congregation only threw salt on open wounds.

It was particularly difficult for several of the clergy I interviewed to remain in the same city as their antagonists.

I gave them what they wanted. I resigned, but they won't leave us alone. My agreement is that my family can live in the rectory until the school session ends for our children. There are certain cars that continually drive by the rectory ever so slowly day and night. Someone came into the house and rifled through the files in my study. No one is supposed to have a key but my wife and me. Obviously that's not true. **A male priest in The Episcopal Church.**

Another priest wrote about receiving an unexpected and unwanted visit at their home from one of their antagonists after they had resigned.

It just feels like such a violation that she would come to our house uninvited. It feels sick and disgusting and dirty...time to just shake the dust! I know that you collect stories, and I had a need to tell someone who would understand so that's the reason for my writing. I'm grateful for your ministry to those of us who have gone through this kind of abuse. **A female priest in The Episcopal Church.**

I've cut all ties with that place. I don't want to hear anything about it or from them. I told them to take me off their mailing list. I still have a lot of friends in that congregation. They want to talk with me about the church. I don't want to hear it. Am I wrong? **A pastor in The United Methodist Church.**

Soon after resigning it appears that it is important to cut all formal ties with the parish to begin the healing process. If there are members that want to maintain a friendship with you just advise them that "church talk" is off limits. Keeping up with the success and or failure of the congregation does not appear to be helpful to the healing process. Getting such reports often served to ignite the memories of the abuse. The clergy and lay leaders I interviewed agreed it was best to put that experience behind them.

Granted when a victim separates from the parish the antagonists will have even more freedom to control the narrative. Even if you were to stay involved it would be difficult to combat their narrative. You have to trust the "truth tellers" that remain in the congregation to respond to the spin of the antagonists.

Accepting harsh realities is not easy, but doing so can assist with healing. Those that believe the spin of the antagonists about your leaving do so because they want to believe it. That is beyond your control. It is at this point the words of the *Serenity Prayer* can bring you comfort. *Accept those things I cannot change.* The good news is that the vast majority of the congregation you served know the truth. They won't believe anything the antagonists have to say. Their words and actions are ever so transparent.

Several pastors reported they found relief by moving to another city or state. If a move was not an alternative all agreed that avoiding so far as possible the establishments most often frequented by parish members was helpful.

I went back and did a quick skim through of "When Sheep Attack." The "it is not about you" conclusion was close to the point I tried to make on the phone call about continuing to monitor healthy and unhealthy parishes online to get an occasional shot of reinforcement! It also caused me to look at another point you made that I actually did to recover but didn't articulate: I/we left the parish. Completely. We paid the rest of our pledge and never returned. Never. I didn't want the children to see adults acting that way. If we had just motored on for a few more months until my term expired and stayed there in the back pews, we probably wouldn't be in any pew today. Leaving was the first step towards recovery. (Sounds like a 12-step program! Hi, I'm N and I used to be a Senior Warden at an unhealthy parish. Funny. And not so funny.) **A male former senior warden in The Episcopal Church.**

For victims of a sheep attack we can conclude that separating from all that might remind them or even renew the pain they have experienced is a healing decision. It was reported that finding a healthy congregation to attend for worship also helped bring healing. Some reported that going to a parish of a different denomination or branch of Christianity was most helpful. It was reported that just being surrounded by healthy people in a healthy congregational system restored and renewed. One former senior warden that had been targeted by the same antagonists as his rector moved his family to a healthy parish. On reflection he asked if he would have gone to any church if his children were not of Sunday School age.

Antagonists are often quite successful in driving a wedge between their victims and the Church. Allowing them to do the same with your relationship with God is also a possibility. Any time a person is targeted by those who believe themselves to be spiritually superior the temptation is to simply walk away from all religion. The God that brought you to ministry is still there. The Almighty has not forgotten you. Both during and after a sheep attack returning to the basics that have nurtured your spiritual life are all the more critical. Walking away from your current parish may help with your healing. Obviously, walking away from an abusive parish does not equate with walking away from God.

2. Victims of a sheep attack have been through a painfully negative experience. The clergy I interviewed intuitively knew that the best way to overcome negative emotions is to replace them with positive ones. The fiftieth Psalm reminds us to offer thanksgiving to God and call upon the Almighty at the time of trouble. The two concurrent admonitions to mix thanksgiving and trouble might appear confusing. Our spiritual mothers and fathers learned early on to bless God even in the day of trouble. To overcome the pain of a sheep attack and find healing involves doing that very thing. These wounded clergy reported

that they tried to begin each morning by reminding themselves of a few things for which they were grateful. *"I told myself every day just how grateful I was that never again in my life would I even have to look at some of those people."* Another reported, *"I begin my prayers with the things and people that cause my cup to overflow."*

Those familiar with the Twelve Steps of Alcoholics Anonymous are aware of a practice called "The Gratitude List". Members of AA and Al Anon find great value in this exercise. Whenever they are tempted to "suck on their thumbs" and throw themselves a "pity party" they counter the negativity with a gratitude list. They simply sit down with a tablet or at their computer and make a list of all their blessings. They list those things and people that fill their lives with thankfulness. They counter the negative by filling their hearts and minds with thanksgiving. Other victims of sheep attacks found value in the meditations found online and readily available on CDs and DVDs. Still others reported that practicing the art of Yoga brought peace and serenity to their lives.

As long as the focus is on the negative and the painful, then the antagonists continue to perform their evil in your life. By calling to the forefront the blessings that surround you, the rotten fruit of their behavior is buried in a deep, deep grave.

It's important to accept that our emotional memories are never erased. They will always be with us. Our task is to replace the negative memories with positive ones. Think of them as being pushed down our memory bank by positive emotional memories. The metaphor I thought of was seeing the opposing team's quarterback in the Super Bowl being piled on by the players of your favorite team. Perhaps a less violent image would be to simply observe that they cease to be available for instant recall. They are outweighed by new positive memories. As any victim of a sheep attack will tell you, however, the right stimulus months or even years later can cause the entire memory to roll back over you like a tsunami. That is all the more reason to pile the positive memories and experiences on top of the negative ones.

3. You will be angry. All the emotions surrounding anger were reported. *"It wasn't fair." "I did nothing to deserve being treated that way." "I got no help from my bishop." "They have destroyed my ministry and no one seems to give a damn."* Anger must be discharged in a positive manner. The anger you feel for having been betrayed is normal, healthy and justified. Denying that anger is dangerous. When a person denies that they are angry and buries it, they do not bury it dead. They bury it alive. It will multiply and become gangrenous. It may express itself

physically. Buried anger may even contribute to a serious illness.

In a healthy relationship the anger can be expressed directly to the person that hurt us. We can use our *"I statements"*. *"I feel ... I hurt ... I am angry."* The direct approach will not work with those that abused us. As has already been shown, they don't believe they've done anything wrong. They were simply *"doing what is best for their church"*. They will tell you that you have no right to be angry or hurt.

Ventilating your anger is the healthiest option in these situations. Some clergy wrote letters that were never mailed. Others reported that journaling their feelings was helpful. To those clergy I offered another word of caution. While journaling or writing letters, don't just focus on your pain and negative feelings. Once again, focus on the positive. Write about the happy moments in the parish and the people that appreciated you and your ministry. Finally, it was consistently reported that physical exercise was a tremendous help. Clergy that had let that part of their physical discipline lapse for years rediscovered the benefits of simply putting their bodies in motion. *"I took a brisk twenty-minute walk each day and it really did do wonders."* I spoke with one Episcopal priest that reported that he'd gained ten pounds of solid muscle in just a few weeks after a sheep attack. He started going to the gym on a regular basis and lifting weights. He stated that he'd never felt better or looked better in his entire life.

    4. It was Anglican author Dorothy Sayer who made the point that there are two types of martyrs. If the pain we experience in life makes us bitter; if we allow pain to harden our hearts and destroy our souls then we become martyrs for the devil. However, if we use the traumas in life to make us more loving, forgiving, and compassionate, then we become martyrs for God. Hurt and anger can be used to fuel ongoing hate and revenge. Or it can be redeemed and those energies can be used to right wrongs and help others.

    One of the most healing things the victims of a sheep attacks reported was that they felt they were more empathetic than ever to the pain of others. I'm not suggesting that they all jumped immediately into volunteering at a homeless shelter or a soup kitchen. I'm not discouraging it either. I'm simply reporting that doing for others lifted them out of their pain. It makes sense. The focus was shifted from their internal wounds to what they could do for others. Simple acts of kindness brought healing.

    Several reported they did not have to look outside their own household. Clergy came to the realization that they had too often been forced to neglect spouse, children, friends and other family members in order to meet the needs of a demanding parish life. All will rejoice to see that changed. Some reported that they had rediscovered their love for art, music, cooking, gardening or recreational reading. Others found they had rediscovered the art of conversation with their family and friends. The bottom line is that all refused to feed the pain the antagonists had brought into their lives. Their focus was on bringing joy and happiness and a little kindness into the lives of the people who loved them, and on occasion, perfect strangers.

Maybe all this is summarized in a bumper sticker I saw. *"Join the Episcopal Church and do random acts of kindness and senseless acts of beauty."* Doing random acts of kindness and senseless acts of beauty can bring healing.

5.   Stay focused on the future. The trauma of the sheep attack is in the past. It is tempting to play *"what if"* and *"I should have"*. *Should of, would of, could of* are words that will drive even the healthiest person into a deep depression. Using those words to look back at the circumstances around your abuse will do just that. Healing is found in the present and the future. Rejoicing in the goodness of each new day brings healing. Making plans and then seeing those plans fulfilled renews our souls. The pastors and other victims found that as long as they focused their energies on the present and future they knew peace. Using *could, would and should* to analyze the events around their

abuse only led to paralysis. Staying present and future oriented is especially helpful in order to counter the nightmares and flashbacks that so many of the victims reported. These often occurred years after the event itself. Sleep would be disturbed with dreams of regret or reoccurrence. An event, symbol or person that reminded them of their abusive experience often stimulated these nightmares. Some of this will be beyond your control. Choosing to leave the past in the past so far as you are able is a healing decision.

Healing Begins

    1. By shaking the dust from your feet and removing yourself from the parish and all that surrounds it.
    2. Burying all the negative, traumatic and painful memories under a host of new, positive and happy ones.
    3. Discharging your anger in a positive manner.
    4. Turning your hurt and pain into acts of love and compassion.
    5. Living in the present and the future. Leave the past in the past.

For Reflection and Discussion

- Do you agree that abused clergy and lay leaders should cut their ties with the parish? Why or why not?

- Do you ever use the "Gratitude List" or some form of it? Explain.

- Years after its occurrence, those that have been abused by antagonists have nightmares about the event. Why do think this is so?

- What other steps can you suggest to assist with the healing of those that have been abused?

"Let them be put to shame and dishonor who seek after my life! Let them be turned back and disappointed who devise evil against me! Let them be like chaff before the wind, with the angel of the Lord driving them away!"
Psalm 35

Chapter 14

One Last Bitter Pill

Without a doubt the words of Jesus about loving our enemies and forgiving our persecutors are some of his most difficult. Yet they are words that victims of a sheep attack must apply if they are to be healed. It is the most bitter medicine that has to be swallowed. It is essential for the healing of all who have gone through this nightmare. This bitter pill applies to senior pastors, lay professionals, board members and members of a wounded congregation. The prescribed medicine in this chapter must be realized for healing to be complete.

I've often taught that forgiving those that have injured us just may be the most difficult work that a Christian has to do. It will be particularly difficult for those that have been bullied and abused. Yet forgiveness is one of the greatest gifts that we can give ourselves. We forgive those that have hurt us for our own emotional, physical and spiritual health.

Wounded Christians, like the general population, are no less tempted to think that withholding forgiveness will punish those that have abused them. It's hard to let go of the memories of the things they said and did. Threats, blackmail, lies and intimidation are not easily forgotten. But therein lies the dilemma. By keeping them alive we don't punish the antagonists. We punish ourselves. When we relive the memories we relive the emotions. The negative emotions bring back the anxiety and fear. With them comes an increase in our heart rhythm, our blood pressure, the production of gastric acid and all the physical reactions, if allowed to continue, will harm our overall health.

It's important to remember the well-known study that was done at Hope College in Holland, Michigan. They asked volunteers to think about someone who had hurt them. As they dwelt on their resentments, the subjects showed greater physiological stress, including more rapid heartbeat and an increase in their blood pressure. Even their facial expressions became distorted. After they were told to stop thinking about the person and the events, the signs of physiological distress did not abate, but continued.

These subjects were then asked to imagine what it would feel like to forgive the person that had hurt them. They reported a more peaceful feeling. They reported that they were happier and more in control. The researchers noted that the physiological systems of the subjects relaxed.

Nurturing anger, resentment, and hurt is self-destructive. Our serenity is not found in focusing on our hurts. A forgiving heart brings peace. Anger and resentment are lethal. Our inner being becomes diseased. The original understanding of the word *disease* had nothing to do with viruses and bacteria. It was defined as a *"dis-ease"* in our souls, our very anima. It meant our total harmony had been destroyed. Resentment destroys our harmony. Grace and forgiveness bring healing and wholeness. Our souls, our very beings, are put in a state of ease. We set ourselves free from those that hurt us. Their words and actions will no longer have any power over us.

I am not going to suggest that this is easy. It may be the most difficult part of the healing process. It will not be accomplished quickly. It will take time. Our Higher Power makes forgiving possible. It is the Almighty's way of restoring hope and healing in our lives. Forgiveness is a process. It can only be accomplished one step at a time. The first step is to make the decision to forgive and set ourselves free from those that hurt us.

In my book, *Forgive and Get Your Life Back,* I give a detailed description of the steps that I believe are included in the forgiveness process. The first step is to find an empathetic ear. This is why I think it important that the victims of sheep attacks seek out others that have also been through the same nightmare. Hearing yourself share your experience and hearing their experience is a critical part of healing. It is my hope that just reading the experiences on the pages of this book will remind you that you are not alone. You are a part of a nightmare shared by a multitude of competent, successful, faithful servants of God. That is the primary reason I've asked some of those for permission to print their stories in these books. It is also critical that every victim of a sheep attack seek out a professional counselor or spiritual director.

I was hurt. I was humiliated. I was too embarrassed to tell anyone what had happened to me. I was so angry with myself that I had not seen it coming, but they were chameleons. I should have known better than to even go to that parish. One of my clergy friends told me they had a reputation. I became so depressed I knew I had to do something. I found a caring counselor. She encouraged me to talk about it. I had to begin by acknowledging just what had happened. The hurt and anger poured out of me. **A female priest in The Episcopal Church.**

As has already been observed, those abused by the antagonists will often share some of the same feelings of embarrassment and shame as victims of physical and sexual abuse. Talking about the experience is the most healing method for transcending those emotions. Pastors place their trust in the integrity of the leaders of the congregation. When trust is betrayed it is tempting to blame oneself for having done so. The betrayal of trust is not information about the one that trusted but the one that abused that trust. Acknowledging their betrayal is an essential step in the forgiveness process.

It is not unusual for a person to blame themselves for being a victim or target of another's sin. Many reported feeling foolish for having trusted the person. This meant they would have a difficult time forgiving themselves for having done so. *"How could I have been so stupid?"* Most of us will feel foolish for having trusted the person that hurt us in any situation of betrayal. This is a tangled web. It means we will have a difficult time forgiving ourselves for someone else's sins. When we are able to reveal our pain to another human being we are able to accept our own humanity. We are not always in control. We are not invincible. We are not perfect. Bringing the experience out in the open and talking about it is critical.

A wise counselor will keep us from judging, belittling or punishing ourselves for trusting. They will remind us over and over that what happened to us is not information about us. Their behavior is information about those that abused us. Just as talking is part of our healing process it must not be unleashed without boundaries. In order to move through the first step in the forgiveness process it is important that we not get stuck in the talking phase. Again, a capable counselor will move us forward.

Forgive and Forget

Forgiving and forgetting is a phrase that sounds hollow when we are hurting. When your heart has literally been ripped from your chest the suggestion that you suddenly develop amnesia is not a very attractive alternative. The first temptation is to make sure no one ever forgets what they did to you and just what kind of person they are. Keeping the experience alive will not hurt your abusers. They are taking pride in what they did. They have established their bragging rights. They see their actions as righteous and holy. The focus needs to be on your healing.

Turning off the video is one of the greatest gifts that we can give ourselves. As long as we keep the video going, we will continue to suffer and agonize over the event. If we allow our minds to follow the hurtful course, we will relive the painful moment again and again. While we will never forget it, we can turn off the reruns. We can choose to leave the event and all the surrounding details, real and imagined, in the past.

In my book, *Forgive and Get Your Life Back,* I use the following story to illustrate this lesson. *I am reminded of the farmer who had a cat that he loved ever so dearly. To the farmer's great grief, the cat died. The farmer gave the cat a proper burial in the flower garden behind his house. However, this burial was unique. The farmer buried the cat, but he left the tail sticking out of the ground. A week or so passed and the farmer began to think about his cat. He decided to go to the burial site to check on the cat. He reached down and grabbed the tail. He pulled the cat out of the ground. He looked at the cat. The cat did not look so well. The cat did not smell very good either. The farmer returned the cat to his final resting place, but again, he left the tail sticking out. Each time the farmer went to the grave and pulled the cat out of the ground, the cat looked worse and smelled worse than it did on the previous viewing.*

It is the same way with our past hurts. As painful as they were at the time, each time we bring them into the present for another viewing, they look worse and they smell worse. In short, they hurt even more than they did initially. To forgive and forget does not mean we develop amnesia. We will never be able to erase the painful offense from our memory. We simply choose to bury it in the past, tail and all.

Reconciliation Is Not An Option

I saw him coming. He had a big smile on his face. His arms were outstretched to hug me. I couldn't believe my eyes. When he approached I put my hand out and pushed it against his chest. I looked him in the eye. He looked surprised. I said very quietly, "I have forgiven you, but I will not hug you." He shrugged his shoulders and walked away. He was one of the four men that had conspired against me. I had thought he was my friend for years only to find out that he was a Judas. The lies that he and the others told about me will never get corrected. They completely destroyed my effectiveness and credibility in that parish. Then he wanted to hug me… really? **A male priest in The Episcopal Church.**

Before we can reconcile with another we have to know that they are truly sorry. We need to hear their words of repentance. We need to know their contrition is genuine. To reconcile with those who are not truly contrite is to excuse their offense as though it never occurred. We in essence put our blessing on their behavior. We shrug our shoulders and pretend it didn't matter. We are basically giving them permission to hurt us again. We need to hear the person who hurt us take responsibility for their behavior.

Those that target clergy are oblivious to the pain they cause others. They have actually deceived themselves into believing they have done the right thing. They are consumed with their public image. Their energies go into maintaining social superiority. They are most concerned about what their social group thinks about them. **I have not found a single case of an antagonist seeking to reconcile with the pastor they targeted for destruction.**

True repentance would also include trying to undue the damage that their conspiracy of lies brought on their pastor. It would mean accepting responsibility for their behavior.

We have to accept the fact that some people will never take responsibility for their action. Some will never come to terms with the pain they have caused. Some will rationalize their acts of sin and evil as righteous and justified. This is especially true if they live with a social or psychological disorder. If Narcissistic Personality Disorder is to be accepted as a possible explanation for this behavior then it will be next to impossible for them to accept responsibility for their actions. It would require intense therapy. People living with this disorder seldom seek therapy and most that do fail to respond to it. Reconciliation is simply not an option. To do so would be to fail to hold them accountable for the pain they have caused. We cannot reconcile with them, but for our soul's sake we still must forgive them.

No Ring, No Robe, No Fatted Calf

Restoration is the fullest expression of forgiveness. The parable of the prodigal son is a parable of restoration. The father forgave, reconciled and restored the prodigal to his former position in his life. To restore the person who hurt us to their former place in our lives is to move forward with them as though they never traumatized us. Restoration is the fullest expression of forgiveness. It requires that the one who hurt us not only be sorry for their sin. It requires that they change their ways. They must make restitution. They must correct, so far as they are able, the damage they have done. Sadly, reconciliation and restoration are both unlikely possibilities in our relationships with antagonists.

Forgiveness is a process of putting the past in the past and leaving it there. We do that for ourselves. Reconciliation requires repentance. The prerequisites for reconciliation with an antagonist are - confession, contrition and amendment.

Restoration requires that the antagonists agree to treatment and rehabilitation. These studies indicate that those intent on attacking clergy, lay ministry professionals and other members of the congregation are incapable of doing either.

Healing Begins

*The first person to apologize is
the bravest.
The first person to forgive is
the strongest.
The first person to forget is
the happiest.*

For Reflection and Discussion

- Do you think it's possible to truly forgive without first hearing yourself verbalize the depth of your hurt and humiliation to another person that understands? Why or why not?

- What are some specific things that you can do to leave the past in the past? Are there symbols or hurtful reminders that you need to remove? Would removing those things help you leave the past in the past?

- If your antagonist were to come to you and ask for forgiveness, what particular words would you want to hear to know that they were truly repentant? What would they need to do to demonstrate their contrition?

- Under what circumstances do you believe a person should restore their abuser to a full relationship in their lives?

*He has shown you, O mortal, what is good.
And what does the Lord require of you?
To act justly and to love mercy
and to walk humbly with your God.*
Micah 6:8

Chapter 15

Remaining In Parish Ministry

I resigned my pastorate five years ago after being viciously attacked by three men and one woman in my last congregation. They were so cruel to my wife she was on the verge of an emotional breakdown. I was in a position to retire so I decided that to be the more desirable choice. Even some of my closest friends in leadership in the congregation were afraid of those four. I found a wonderful new church in our chosen retirement community. Last Sunday that same group visited my new church home. They attended a social and engaged my fellow church members. They attacked my character. They told people that they had fired me for incompetence. I retired because I didn't want to do battle with them any longer. Doctor Maynard, they traveled over one hundred miles for the sole purpose of discrediting me in my new church home. **A male priest in The Episcopal Church**

Pastors that have resigned following a sheep attack have to live with the reality that their antagonists will continue to try to destroy their ministry. They will be marked as a reject. The antagonists delight in bragging that they were *"fired"*. Deployment officers, bishops and denominational executives will more often than not stamp your résumé with a stamp - *not suitable for ministry*. I long for the day that the leadership of every congregation will be educated on this phenomenon. It will be a new day when search committees, vestries and boards can look at a candidate and remark, *"So you experienced a sheep attack. We know all about that and we don't need the details. We want to talk about the gifts God has given you and how you might use them in this congregation."*

Until that day my research indicates that abused clergy that want to remain in parish ministry have three possible avenues. The first is to seek out a bishop or denominational officer who understands the dynamics of a sheep attack and wants to help you find a position. The second is to find a senior pastor of a large congregation who also understands sheep attacks. They can consider employing you as an associate. The third avenue is interim ministry. Some clergy have found that interim ministry can lead to being called as the senior pastor of the congregation they are serving as interim. Before moving into another position as a senior pastor, every clergy person should evaluate carefully if they are physically, emotionally and spiritually ready to do so.

Once again I want to offer a particular word of caution to any lay professional or pastor who has been diagnosed with burnout or post traumatic stress injury. At the risk of repeating myself, there were enough reported cases of clergy that did so to emphasize it one more time. Based on the cases I reviewed it may be ill advised for a burned out or PTSD victim to immediately re-enter parish ministry as a senior pastor. It may be ill advised to ever to do so. Recovering from burnout or PTSD takes time. Burnout is not easily overcome in a few days, weeks or even months. The haunting memories associated with a post traumatic stress injury can last for decades. Clergy all know that the life of a senior pastor in most any congregation is taxing. Severely wounded clergy are advised not to ignore that reality.

Warning Signs Not To Ignore

Victims of a sheep attack simply must not ignore certain warning signs. One of the most urgent is lingering depression. If you find yourself metaphorically in a dark hole and simply have no energy for your daily routine, seek help immediately. The same can be said for those that find their sleep routinely disturbed by nightmares and flashbacks of the event. If you frequently wake in the middle of the night in a cold sweat remembering the abuse, therapy is the first line of treatment. If you continue to be embarrassed by the nightmare that was thrust upon you, it must be verbalized.

Disassociation is particularly dangerous. This is particularly true if you feel like you are looking back on the event as though it has happened to someone else. Professional help must be sought as soon as possible.

Again, I ask you to think of the victims of sexual or domestic abuse and the shame and humiliation they experienced. Victims of sheep attacks often share those same emotions. The only hope for healing is to open their pain to a qualified therapist. The memory of the trauma will never go away. With proper treatment the painful aftershocks can be minimized. Trusting again may be one of the most difficult tasks. Betrayed by the very people they once trusted, victims of a sheep attack become overly cautious. They will find trusting anyone again a challenge, but it is a challenge that can be met.

An Alternative Profession

Several of the clergy I interviewed found that the best way they could remain in ministry was to pursue an alternative career. This was easiest for pastors that were returning to a prior profession they had practiced before ordination. They were often able to continue in parish ministry as volunteer associates in a congregation. Those clergy that are without other professional degrees or experience found the path more difficult. Putting *"Minister of the Gospel"* on their résumé did not make them very marketable. However, with the assistance of professional résumé writers they discovered new career opportunities. Consider the skills and experience of a typical parish pastor. First, you've conquered what most people consider to be their number one fear. You are able to speak before a group of people without a quivering voice or shaking knees. But consider all the skills you had to develop to simply lead a parish. You had to work with boards, supervise volunteers and often paid staff. You had to develop the ability to plan, budget and then manage a budget. You had to manage a physical plant, grounds, repairs and scheduling. Fundraising, marketing skills, writing and editing materials for publication are all thrown in the mix. And of course, these are but a few of the skills and experience any endeavor in the marketplace will find valuable in a potential employee. If continuing in full time parish ministry is not advisable or an option, all doors are not closed. You have so much to offer. All is not lost. A professional résumé writer could prove to be one of your better investments. Continuing as a pastor may require that you utilize some of that same creativity that brought such success to the congregations you've served.

After I resigned my last parish I was certain that I never wanted another. My problem was that I loved being a pastor. Our local hospital was without a chaplain. I met with the administrator and asked if I could serve as their chaplain on a volunteer basis.

There were certain conditions he insisted that I agree to, like not prosthelytizing. When I assured him I did not have a parish nor did I plan to start one, he was greatly relieved. The long and short of it is that after just a few short months, he was miraculously able to find the funds to employ me full time. I am a pastor without a parish, true. But I am a pastor and none of the patients I care for have ever attacked me or questioned my character. Some are irritable. Others are impatient. A few are just downright cranky. None have come close to exhibiting the cruel behavior I experienced in that dysfunctional parish. Thanks for writing "When Sheep Attack". And thanks for being my pastor. **A male pastor in a non-denominational Church.**

Healing Begins

This is one of the toughest parts of the healing process for victims of a sheep attack. Each minister must decide whether or not they will maintain a relationship with a worshipping community.

I discovered those that have decided they want none. Others have a sporadic relationship at best. Some have developed new and creative ministries for themselves. Still others remain quite active as volunteer Sunday assistants. Then there are those that entered full time interim ministry and those that sought and found full time parish responsibility.

It appears that this is clearly a decision that cannot be categorized as "one size fits all". Each pastor must discern for themselves the type of ongoing relationship they will have with a congregation. That which will bring healing is at the very heart of their decision.

For Reflection and Discussion

- Do you think clergy that have been subjected to a sheep attack should advise any search committee of that fact? Why or why not?

- If you were on a search committee charged with calling a new senior pastor, would evidence of a sheep attack cause you to remove them from consideration? Why or why not?

- Should all clergy maintain an alternative career option? Why or why not?

- What are some of the things you would add to a pastor's résumé to make them more marketable in the secular job world?

"Therefore, if anyone is in Christ, the new creation has come. The old has gone. The new is here!"
2 Corinthians 5:17

Chapter 16

Recovery and Resurrection

Every person, lay and ordained, can receive inspiration from the determination to proclaim the gospel exhibited by John Wesley. At that time the leaders of the Church opposed his ministry. In his diary he wrote:

"Sunday, A.M., May 5: Preached in St. Anne's. Was asked not to come back anymore...

Sunday, P.M., May 5: Preached in St. John's. Wardens said "Get out and stay out...

Sunday, A.M., May 12: Preached in St. Jude's. Can't go back there, either...

Sunday, A.M., May 19: Preached in St. Somebody Else's. Wardens called special meeting and said I couldn't return...

Sunday, P.M., May 19: Preached on street. Kicked off the street...

Sunday, A.M., May 26: Preached in meadow. Chased out of meadow as bull was turned loose during service...

Sunday, A.M., June 2: Preached out at the edge of town. Kicked off the highway...

Sunday, P.M., June 2: Afternoon, preached in a pasture. Ten thousand people came out to hear me."

From these studies there is one impression that has left an endearing mark on my soul. In all the cases I've studied, the attacked clergy, religious professionals and lay leaders have chosen to take the high road. I can find no evidence of any of them using the Internet to defame their attackers or parish.

Several of the contributors to my work were anxious that I not be "unkind" or "judgmental" in describing the behaviors of their antagonists. They needed me to remain "objective" and "analytical" but not be "harsh". The pastoral calling runs deep. I fear the same cannot be said for the "anonymous" antagonists. The high road appears to be something beyond their reach. I hope that does not sound harsh, judgmental or unkind. The evidence leads to that conclusion and that is factual. It appears they will continue to malign and defame the very clergy they've attacked until their dying breath.

Granted I am not an attorney, but from the cases I've studied, I believe there were multiple opportunities to file litigation against the attackers. The overwhelming majority of victims have thus far chosen not to do so. I was discussing all this with one of the members of the panel I used to review this book. He reminded me of the following passages from the Book of Romans the twelfth chapter. It is a fitting conclusion to a book intended to help bringing healing for those that have been attacked by antagonists.

Bless those who persecute you, bless and do not curse. Do not repay anyone evil for evil. Do not take revenge, my dear friends, but leave room for God's wrath, for it is written: "It is mine to avenge; I will repay," says the Lord.

On the contrary: If your enemy is hungry, feed him; if he is thirsty, give him something to drink. In doing this, you will heap burning coals on his heard. Do not be overcome by evil, but overcome evil with good.

Recovering from a sheep attack is a resurrection. The recovery process provides you with the opportunity for a new life. There is the opportunity to re-evaluate. That is one of the gifts this horrible experience offers you. It is the grace in the entire situation. With the help of a mental health professional and a good spiritual director you can return to the basics. What really fulfills you? What makes you happy? Having lived through a sheep attack, is God calling you to a new or different kind of ministry? These are all positive possibilities.

"I know that they thought they had destroyed me, but in a strange way they actually did me a favor. Because I had been so stressed at the church my marriage was also stressed. I was too tired even to play with my children when I got home. In my last *parish I was constantly running around putting out fires. I'm not running a parish any longer, but I have time for my wife and my family. I feel appreciated at work. I feel like I am really helping people. I am actually experiencing more love and appreciation in the "big, bad, greedy corporation" I now work for than I did in the Church. I've also lost thirty pounds and my doctor has taken me off my blood pressure medication. I couldn't be happier.* **A male priest in The Episcopal Church.**

There is a familiar expression. *Pain is inevitable. Misery is optional.* The pain that was thrust on you was not your choosing. The quality of life and ministry you have following the nightmare is your choice. Choose to be happy. It will drive your antagonists crazy.

Living through a sheep attack will bring you to the turning point in your life when you can simply walk away from drama and all the people that thrive on it. You can give priority to people that make you laugh and bring smiles to your face at the very mention of their names. You can bury the bad memories of the past and leave them there. The memoires of the moments of joy with the beautiful people in your life are the ones you can choose to keep alive. You can hold closest the people who you love and love you in return. Walking away from the people who want to treat you badly becomes easier and easier. Living through a sheep attack provides you with the opportunity to choose happiness.

I want to end these observations on recovering from a sheep attack where I began. The experience that was thrust on you is **not information about you.** It is, however, information about your antagonists and the congregational players in the system. The people who loved you and appreciated your ministry will continue to do so. The ministry achievements that you put in place that are beyond the antagonist's ability to dismantle will remain. If they continue to attack and discredit you they only reveal their true selves. More and more people will come to terms with the bitter fruit of their work. Allow me to repeat - *you never need to explain yourself. Your friends don't require an explanation and your enemies won't believe anything you say*. Clergy, lay professionals and lay leaders that have lived through a sheep attack know the truth of that axiom all too well. Those they once thought to be friends quickly believe the spin the antagonists put on your leaving. Your friends, however, will continue to be your friends.

It is also important to realize that you are wounded because you gave your all. Many people caught in the *"damned if I do and damned if I don't"* would bail out at the first indication. The fact that you endured for as long as you did means that you took your responsibility for the sheep given into your care seriously. *The depression, anxiety and exhaustion you now feel are not a sign of weakness. They are but a sign of having tried to remain strong far too long.* Your battle scars are evidence that you did all you could do to be a faithful shepherd. You are not a hireling.

I am not suggesting that enduring a sheep attack is the purple heart of ministry, but I am asking you to accept the fact that you did all that you could do. The words of the prophet Isaiah offer the following promise. *"The Lord shall renew your strength; you shall mount up with wings as eagles; you shall run, and not be weary; and you shall walk, and not faint."*

It is my prayerful hope that one or more of the stories I've shared with you in this book has brought comfort to those that have been subjected to an attack. While no one wants to be a member of this club it can be comforting to realize that you are not the only one. The nightmare you lived as a senior minister, lay professional or lay leader is not information about you! You did nothing wrong!

The nightmare that was thrust on you was not your doing. It could happen to anyone. I further pray that reading the dynamics of the attacks common to every brand of religion will assist with your healing. After studying the psychological profile of antagonists I hope you can accept that, alone, there was nothing you could do. When the denominational leaders, the vestry or board, and the matriarchs and patriarchs of the parish join with you in simply telling them to *"knock it off"*, **then - and only then will the antagonists be disarmed**.

Healing Begins

A few years ago, at the invitation of the then current rector, I returned to one of the congregations that I'd served. It was an anniversary celebration. I found the members of the parish anxious to reminisce about the time we were together. Their walks down memory lane were most interesting. They did not want to recall the wonderful programs we put together for Advent and Lent. None mentioned the spectacular worship services, the successful stewardship drives, the capital campaigns or my insightful sermons (sigh). The litany of memories followed this pattern. *"You baptized our children." "You performed our wedding. Our children want to meet you." "You helped me get a job." "You were there when my dad was dying." "You came to see me before my surgery. I was so scared."*

Jesus called you to a ministry that would bear fruit. He described it as a fruit that would last. The antagonists will never be able to destroy the tender moments when you were able to be pastor and priest to those in your care. Simply by your prayers and presence you reminded those in grief or pain that God was with them. During their joyful moments in life they will never forget that you were with them as they exchanged vows, presented their children for baptism and confirmation, and blessed the transitional moments in their lives. Your antagonists have tried to destroy you and your ministry. **They have failed!** In the hearts and memories of those that you served you will always be there. They will never forget it. Yours was a ministry that will live on forever with those that allowed you to be their pastor. Your ministry will live on in their hearts and minds. It is God's promise.

A Cherokee Parable

An old Cherokee chief was teaching his grandson about life... "A fight is going on inside me," he said to the boy. "It is a terrible fight and it is between two wolves. One is evil - he is anger, envy, sorrow, regret, greed, arrogance, self-pity, guilt, resentment, inferiority, lies, false pride, superiority, self-doubt and ego. The other is good - he is joy, peace, love, hope, serenity, humility, kindness, benevolence, empathy, generosity, truth, compassion and faith. This same fight is going on inside you - and inside every person, too."

The grandson thought about it for a minute and then asked his grandfather, "Which wolf will win?"

The old chief simply replied, "The one you feed."

Author Unknown.

For Reflection and Discussion

- Why do you think more clergy don't file litigation against their abusers?

- Why do you think it is so difficult for bishops and denominational leaders to confront antagonists and to simply tell them to "knock it off"?

- Name a few people in your congregations that allowed you to be their pastor. List some of the spirit-filled moments with them that no antagonists will ever be able to destroy?

- Do you agree that the antagonists have failed to destroy you and your ministry? Why or why not?

*"When I sit down to write a book,
I do not say to myself,
'I am going to produce a work of art'.
I write it because there is
some lie that I want to expose,
some fact to which
I want to draw attention,
and
my initial concern is to get a hearing."*

George Orwell

ABOUT THE AUTHOR

The Reverend Doctor Dennis R. Maynard is a best selling author of fourteen books. Well over 150,000 Episcopalians have read his book, *Those Episkopols.* 3,000 congregations around the United States use *Those Episkopols* in their new member ministries. It has been called the unofficial handbook for the Episcopal Church by several bishops and denominational leaders. He is also the author of *Forgive and Get Your Life Back.* Over two thousand clergy have used that book to do forgiveness training in their congregations.

Maynard has written a series of novels focusing on life in the typical congregation. These novels have received popular acceptance from both clergy and lay people. The seven books in *The Magnolia Series* are growing in popularity around the nation as readers anxiously await each new chapter.

"The novels give us a chance to look at the underside of parish life. While the story lines are fictional, the readers invariably think they recognize the characters. If not, they know someone just like the folks that attend First Episcopal Church in the town of Falls City, Georgia."

His book, *"When Sheep Attack",* is based on twenty-five case studies of clergy that were attacked by a small group of antagonists. The antagonists successfully removed their senior pastor, leaving the congregations divided and crippled. The book describes how it happened, what could have been done to stop it, and what can be done to prevent it from happening to your pastor and parish.

Over his thirty-eight years of parish ministry he has served some of the largest congregations in the Episcopal Church. He served parishes in Illinois, Oklahoma, South Carolina, Texas, and California. President George H.W. Bush and his family are members of the congregation he served in Houston, Texas, also the largest parish in the Episcopal Church.

He has served other notable leaders that represent the diversity of his ministry. These national leaders include Former Secretary of State James Baker; Former Secretary of Education Richard Riley; Supreme Court Nominee Clement Haynsworth and the infamous baby doctor Benjamin Spock, among others.

Doctor Maynard maintains an extensive speaking and travel schedule. Schools, parishes, and organizations throughout the United States regularly call on him to speak, lead retreats, or serve as a consultant.

He was ordained a priest at the age of twenty-four. His first parish assignments were as the curate at Grace Church and vicar of Saint Philip's Mission in Muskogee, Oklahoma. The bishop of the diocese charged him with closing Saint Philip's, a declining African American congregation, and merging it with Grace

Church. At the close of his first year the merger was realized.

He was then called to Saint Mark's Mission in Dallas, Texas. In less than a year the mission achieved parish status. One year later, he successfully led the merger of that parish with nearby Saint Margaret's Parish in Richardson, Texas. Church of the Epiphany was the name chosen by the congregation for the merged parish.

Over the next eight years they grew to a parish averaging one thousand people in attendance at five Sunday services including a service in Mandarin. Under his leadership the congregation held three capital campaigns. One campaign was held to build a new church with a pipe organ, another to remodel the old nave into a parish hall, and one to build a parish life center.

The congregation started a counseling center, a bookstore and a day school. It also became one of the centers for a teen drug abuse program and built a block partnership with an African American Congregation in South Dallas. Church of the Epiphany adopted two large Vietnamese Refugee Families. They brought them to Dallas and helped them begin new and productive lives. The parish was recognized for its growth and ministry in a 1978 article in *The Episcopalian,* the national newspaper for The Episcopal Church.

At the age of thirty-four Dennis Maynard was called to Christ Church and School in

Greenville, South Carolina. At the time Christ Church was the seventh largest congregation in The Episcopal Church in America. Under his leadership it grew to be the fourth largest with six Sunday services.

During his tenure the congregation set up four not for profit corporations. Each was organized to start a Food Bank, a soup kitchen, a free medical clinic, and a house for homeless men living with HIV and AIDS. The parish also built four Habitat For Humanity Houses while he was rector. Along with the diocese the people of Christ Church worked with the Bishop of Haiti on several projects to meet the needs of the people of that diocese.

At the time Maynard went to Greenville, Christ Church Episcopal School was in decline. The school was being heavily subsidized by the parish budget. This was negatively impacting the growth and ministry programs in the congregation. Conversations were held among the leadership about closing the high school since more students were withdrawing from the school than were enrolling in it. Maynard and the head of school at the time began an aggressive student recruitment and marketing campaign. Together they established a board of visitors and an annual fund for the school. In just two years the decline was reversed and the school began to grow.

Maynard led two capital campaigns to expand and improve the facilities for the parish and school at the downtown campus and broke ground for a new middle school building. The campaigns also allowed for the expansion of the downtown campus property.

The parish established a bookstore, a preschool and a counseling center under his leadership. The diocese had made the decision to close one of the mission churches in Greenville. He asked the bishop to make it a chapel of the parish to see if it couldn't be turned around. Saint Andrew's congregation became a self-supporting parish in just three years.

Maynard left Christ Church to become the Vice Rector of the largest congregation in The Episcopal Church, Saint Martin's in Houston, Texas. While there he was able to establish "The Seabury Institute Southwest" as a regional campus for Seabury Theological School in Chicago. Clergy and lay leaders studied for advanced degrees in congregational development through the Institute.

Three years later the bishop and calling committee of Saint James by the Sea Parish in La Jolla, California approached him about becoming their rector. The bishop and vestry at the time were particularly concerned about the declining attendance and finances of the parish. The parish was bleeding its endowment for daily operations and was quite literally living from bequest to bequest. Doctor Maynard believed himself called to be their rector.

He was instrumental in discovering and convicting a long time employee of the parish that had been embezzling large sums of money. He worked with the vestry to establish internal controls and audits to prevent a re-occurrence. They established a separate board to safeguard the endowment of the parish. The pledge budget tripled in just three years. During his tenure the parish also built up an operating reserve to meet projected obligations.

The congregation experienced rapid growth, often filling the four Sunday services. A very successful bookstore and gift shop was established. He also led a capital campaign to address the deferred maintenance issues facing the historic property. The plan included provisions for making the property accessible to people living with physical disabilities. An international Anglican magazine carried an article on the turnaround at St. James by the Sea.

After thirty-eight years of parish ministry Doctor Maynard retired in 2005 to be of service to clergy and congregations in the larger Church. He has worked as a consultant with bishops, clergy, schools and congregations in thirty-one dioceses in the United States and Canada. He has authored fourteen books. They are being used in the congregations of all denominations in the United States, Canada and England. Two of his books are currently being utilized as source material for students in theological schools.

Doctor Maynard's ministry has included service on several diocesan boards and committees. These included various diocesan program committees, director of summer camps for boys, diocesan trustee, finance committees, and executive committees. He was elected Dean of various diocesan deaneries on several occasions. He was on the Cursillo secretariat and was spiritual director for the Cursillo Movement multiple times. Maynard served as co-chair for two diocesan capital campaigns.

In the National Episcopal Church he served multiple terms on the board of the National Association of Episcopal Schools and as a trustee for Seabury Western Theological Seminary. He was named an adjunct professor in congregational development at Seabury. Maynard was the co-coordinator for two national conferences for large congregations with multiple staff ministries.

Doctor Maynard was twice named to "Oxford's Who's Who The Elite Registry of Extraordinary Professionals" and to "Who's Who Among Outstanding Americans".

Maynard has earned four academic degrees. He holds an Associate of Arts Degree in psychology, a Bachelor of Arts Degree in the social sciences, a Masters Degree in theology, and a Doctor of Ministry Degree in Congregational Development. His doctoral thesis was written on systems theory as it applies to congregations in conflict.

He currently resides in Rancho Mirage, California with his wife, Nancy, and their "daughter's cat", Lila. They have raised four children. They are the proud grandparents of one granddaughter and two grandsons.

BOOKS BY DENNIS R. MAYNARD

THOSE EPISKOPOLS
This is a popular resource for clergy to use in their new member ministries. It seeks to answer the questions most often asked about the Episcopal Church. Questions like: "Can You Get Saved in the Episcopal Church?" "Why Do Episcopalians Reject Biblical Fundamentalism?" "Does God Like All That Ritual?" "Are There Any Episcopalians in Heaven?" And others.

FORGIVEN, HEALED AND RESTORED
This book is devoted to making a distinction between forgiving those who have injured us and making the decision to reconcile with them or restore them to their former place in our lives.

THE MONEY BOOK
The primary goal of this book is to present some practical teachings on money and Christian Stewardship. It also encourages the reader not to confuse their self-worth with their net worth.

FORGIVE AND GET YOUR LIFE BACK
This book teaches the forgiveness process to the reader. It's a popular resource for clergy and counselors to use to do forgiveness training. In this book, a clear distinction is made between forgiving, reconciling, and restoring the penitent person to their former position in our lives.

WHEN SHEEP ATTACK
Your rector is bullied, emotionally abused and then his ministry is ended. Your parish is left divided. Formerly faithful members no longer attend. This book is based on the case studies of twenty-five clergy who had just such an experience. What could have been done? What can you do to keep it from happening to you and your parish? Discussion questions are included that make it suitable for study groups.

PREVENTING A SHEEP ATTACK
This is a book that clergy and lay leaders can use to train and educate their leadership on ways to prevent a sheep attack. It explains allowing a sheep attack to occur means that it is inevitable that someone will be ejected from the congregational system. Parish and denominational leaders must choose.

HEALING FOR PASTORS & PEOPLE FOLLOWING A SHEEP ATTACK
If you are a senior minister, music minister, minister of education or faithful lay leader that still suffers with the wounds inflicted on you by a handful of antagonists, this book will assist you with your healing. If years later you still wake in a cold sweat shaking from a nightmare filled with abusive memories, this book can help you. If you feel empty spiritually and unappreciated by the very Church you felt called to serve, this book will comfort you.

THE MAGNOLIA SERIES

BEHIND THE MAGNOLIA TREE (BOOK ONE)
Meet The Reverend Steele Austin. He is a young Episcopal priest who receives an unlikely call to one of the most prestigious congregations

in the Southern United States. Soon his idealism conflicts with the secrets of sex, greed, and power at historic First Church. His efforts to minister to those living with AIDS and HIV bring him face to face with members of the Klu Klux Klan. Then one of the leading members seeks his assistance in coming to terms with the double life he's been living. The ongoing ministry of conflict with the bigotry and prejudice that are in the historic fabric of the community turn this book into a real page-turner.

<u>WHEN THE MAGNOLIA BLOOMS (BOOK TWO)</u>

In this the second book in the Magnolia Series, Steele Austin finds himself in the middle of a murder investigation. In the process the infidelity of one of his closest priest friends is uncovered. When he brings an African American priest on the staff, those antagonistic to his ministry find even more creative methods to rid themselves of the young idealist. Then a most interesting turn of events changes the African American priest's standing in the parish. A young associate undermines the rector by preaching a gospel of hate, alienating most of the women in the congregation and all the gay and lesbian members. The book closes with a cliffhanger that will leave the reader wanting another visit to Falls City, Georgia.

<u>PRUNING THE MAGNOLIA (BOOK THREE)</u>

Steele Austin's vulnerability increases even further when he uncovers a scandal that will shake First Church to its very foundation. In order to expose the criminal, he must first prove his own innocence. This will require him to challenge his very own bishop. The sexual sins of the wives of one of the parish leaders present a most unlikely pastoral opportunity for the rector. In the face of the ongoing attacks of his antagonists, Steele Austin is given the opportunity to leave First Church for a thriving parish in Texas.

THE PINK MAGNOLIA (BOOK FOUR)
The Rector's efforts to meet the needs of gay teenagers that have been rejected by their own families cast a dark cloud over First Church. A pastoral crisis with a former antagonist transforms their relationship into one of friendship. The Vestry agrees to allow the Rector to sell the church owned house and purchase his own, but not all in the congregation approve. The reader is given yet another view of church politics. The book ends with the most suspense filled cliffhanger yet.

THE SWEET SMELL OF MAGNOLIA (BOOK FIVE)
The fifth book in the Magnolia Series follows the Rector's struggle with trust and betrayal in his own marriage. His suspicions about his wife take a heavy toll on his health and his ministry. He brings a woman priest on the staff in face of the congregation's objections to doing so. Some reject her ministry totally. Then the internal politics of the Church are exposed even further with the election of a Bishop. Those with their own agenda manipulate the election itself. Just when you think the tactics of those opposed to the ministry of Steele Austin can't go any lower, they do.

THE MAGNOLIA AT SUNRISE (BOOK SIX)
The lives of The Reverend Steele Austin and the people of First Church face new challenges.

Father Austin takes his sabbatical time to examine his life's purpose. Still stinging from the most recent attacks on his wife and himself from the antagonists in his congregation, he wrestles with the decision as to whether or not he wants to return to First Church. He is even uncertain if he wants to remain in the priesthood.

THE CHANGING MAGNOLIA (BOOK SEVEN)

The masters of the great plantations ruled over those they believed to be inferior to them. Their descendants often believe they are entitled to this same position. With divine right they appeal to their wealth and bloodline, demanding that the unimportant in their world be subservient to them. In Falls City, Georgia those in positions of superiority utilize intimidation, slander, blackmail, sex and even murder to get their way. In this seventh visit to Historic First Church these powerful people have used their influence to destroy the spirit of their own pastor and his family.

All of Doctor Maynard's books can be viewed and ordered on his website.
www.Episkopols.com

Discounts on most of his books are available through his website.

Visit Amazon.com to discover Doctor Maynard's books that are on Kindle.
www.Amazon.com

Dionysus Publications

www.Episkopols.com

Books For Clergy And The People They Serve.

Printed in Great Britain
by Amazon